LEARN TO PLAY

>>> Designing Tutorials for Video Games <<<

LEARN TO PLAY

⋙ Designing Tutorials for Video Games ⋘

Matthew M. White

CRC Press
Taylor & Francis Group
Boca Raton London New York

CRC Press is an imprint of the
Taylor & Francis Group, an **informa** business

AN A K PETERS BOOK

CRC Press
Taylor & Francis Group
6000 Broken Sound Parkway NW, Suite 300
Boca Raton, FL 33487-2742

First issued in hardback 2017

© 2014 by Taylor & Francis Group, LLC
CRC Press is an imprint of Taylor & Francis Group, an Informa business

No claim to original U.S. Government works

Version Date: 20140630

ISBN-13: 978-1-4822-2019-3 (pbk)
ISBN-13: 978-1-138-42766-2 (hbk)

Library of Congress Cataloging-in-Publication Data

White, Matthew M.
  Learn to play : designing tutorials for video games / Matthew M. White.
    pages cm
  Includes bibliographical references and index.
  ISBN 978-1-4822-2019-3 (paperback)
  1. Video games--Handbooks, manuals, etc. I. Title.

GV1469.3.W55 2014
794.8--dc23   2014007205

Visit the Taylor & Francis Web site at
http://www.taylorandfrancis.com

and the CRC Press Web site at
http://www.crcpress.com

Copyright Notices and Limitations

Contents

Preface

There has been a lot of discussion in the last decade about games that teach people something or other. These are mostly excellent books, with people like Gee and Squire really spearheading our curiosity into how games might make people think about things, whether it is playing *Civilization*™ and thinking about the ascent of humanity, or playing *Shadow of the Colossus*™ and really thinking about protagonist roles in literature. With years of heavy research going into this area, surely we have come to realize that games really do make people think.

However, I would like to throw my hat into the ring and say that we have focused almost primarily on how games can teach people how to do other things or to think about other things. We are looking for transfer, some evidence that playing *Civilization* really did get someone interested in history, or *Trauma Center* in surgery, *Phoenix Wright* in law, and so on. While it is important for educators, particularly educational policymakers, to see that playing *Sim City* or *Minecraft* might really get people interested in civil engineering, city planning, or construction, it is not really important for game designers. Let's be honest—we want our players to be moved and changed by our games, but the vehicle through which we do that is fun. Now, what is fun? Well, people like Raph Koster have *amazing* answers to that question, but it is beyond the scope of my book.

What I am going to talk about is how games teach us about themselves. They do this through tutorials. Before reading, I want you to throw out what you think I mean by tutorial. Literally delete every record of it from your brain, supposing that requires a hammer and an ice-cream scoop. This is not a book about how to make a compelling tutorial level: there is no such thing. Rather, it is about how to embed a tutorial directly into your game design mechanics so that your games naturally and comfortably teach new players to have fun.

I hope that by the time you finish the book, you will understand how educators and psychologists help people to learn things. One thing I have learned through my education and experiences with game design and teaching is that education transcends disciplinary boundaries. It is one part science and one part art; one part skilled trade and one part academic. This book will help you understand the science of how people learn things through an understanding of the brain and mind. It will also help you understand the art of teaching things to people by understanding these concepts. More importantly, it will help you design game mechanics, or tutorials, that *teach* people how to have fun with your game.

I hope you find this book useful, informative, and fun!

Acknowledgments

For the steadfast support of my partner Katie and my family.
Peter Kalmar for his amazing artwork.
Penn State, for having an amazing framework that allows me to
continue designing games, writing books, and doing what I love.

About the Author

Matthew White was born in Sydney, Nova Scotia, Canada. Early on, he developed an interest in games, computers, and people watching. From this, he pursued an education in pedagogy, psychology, and game design. Dr. White's undergraduate degrees were completed at Cape Breton University and Memorial University of Newfoundland and focused on, oddly enough, English, Canadian history, drama, and education. After spending some time as a high school teacher using digital games to teach English and drama, he became interested in the motivational properties of video games and, of course, in making them. He completed a Master's degree in instructional design focusing on the design of games from the University of New Brunswick, and completed a Ph.D. in education from Memorial University of Newfoundland, co-supervised through York University's Education and Game Studies faculty. He worked variously designing interfaces, and studied human-computer interaction and game programming through employment at the University of Prince Edward Island and a small indie studio in Charlottetown, PEI, called *Snow Day Games*. More recently, Dr. White has taken employment at Penn State University's Behrend Campus in Erie, PA, where he teaches game design, computer science, and software engineering. He also home-brews a lot of beer and makes video games, as you might imagine.

1

INTRODUCTION

Video Games

If you are reading this book, chances are you are in some way involved in their creation, appreciation, or consumption. They touch all of our lives in one way or another, compelling us to play for hours and hours, providing us an income, or making us write angry letters to the editor. How we perceive games, how we play them, and most importantly, whether or not we enjoy them is guided heavily by our psychology. That said, you don't need a degree in psychology to make good video games. Shigeru Miyamoto showed us that with the right combination of creativity and zaniness, you can mold an entire industry and have a meaningful and profound impact on literally hundreds of millions of people. Similarly, you don't need a degree in psychology to train a dog: take a look at a professional dog trainer, for example. She uses techniques to make man's best friend just a little more friendly. The one thing that binds these people is that both Miyamoto and the trainer are making use of psychological principles to serve a purpose—whether that purpose is to entertain us or make our dogs better companions.

Let me start by saying that reading this book is in no way a good substitute for having a degree in psychology/education/human factors. The knowledge I am going to give you here will just scratch the surface of all of these disciplines, but will do it in such a way that it is relative to game design, and peppered with enough explanation and relation to game mechanics to be directly implemented in your games. In this book, I am going to let all of you in on some secrets. Not in the "self-help book" secrets kind of way, but rather, I am going to link game design principles with psychology through something we are all familiar with and that most of us despise: the game tutorial.

Like the dog trainer analogy, we often make a critical mistake when making games or activities for our players; namely, players don't come with predestined knowledge of how to play your game, nor do puppies come housebroken. In the current games industry, we have been spoiled. We have a large demographic of players who have knowledge of something called *genre*. This might be your first time reading something based in cognitive psychology, or you might read on the topic all the time. In either case, we as humans have a habit of categorizing things through something called a *schema*. We sort things so that our minds can easily manage them. A sparrow is a sort of bird, which is a sort of animal, which is a sort of living thing, and so on. With these schema distinctions, we associate *rules*. Birds can be fed, for example. The bottom line that we tend to miss is that we had to learn these schemas at some point. Just like game players know that shooters often have a reload button, we know that birds will often fly away when approached. The important distinction we often miss, however, is that both gamers and children had to learn these from someone, or something, at some point in their lives. The sort of organization the mind undertakes can be seen in Figure 1.1.

In the childhood of individuals who grew up alongside the games industry, like me and many other people born between 1965 and 1990, games taught us by starting with simple controls. We cut our teeth on the Atari 2600™ with its one button before gradually moving on to the NES with two, the SNES with six, and so on. We learned simple controls like moving objects on the screen in games like *Pac-Man*™,

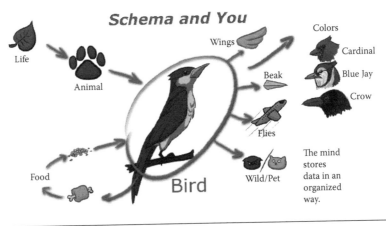

Figure 1.1   Schema diagram. (Figure courtesy of Peter Kalmar.)

and we associated a new schema of control with the objects our hands were touching. Over time, we altered this schema by adding new buttons as modifiers like holding a button to run in games like *Super Mario Bros.*™. This gradual, invisible process, occurring over literally years of playership, trained us to become the gamers we are today. Problematically, new players lack the decades of experience "core" gamers have gathered, and therefore enter the games industry as novices. Worse, still, when these players are drawn to simpler (controller-wise) games on smartphones, *Facebook*, or elsewhere, we alienate and chastise them as *casuals*, a word that has certainly earned infamy on the Internet, at the very least. This entitled behavior of xenophobic exclusion of new gamers only stands to beat the games industry down to a niche market before it finally fades away.

The luxury of being a game designer in the current generation affords us the windfall of having a very, *very*, educated audience. Many gamers consume games like nothing else, taking to message boards and discussion groups to talk about their love, or hate, of their cherished hobby. To our detriment, however, we often approach new players as enigmas. How on Earth do we get new players to actually play our games? If we use heavy-handed tutorials, we risk alienating (read: boring) our "core" audience; however, if we use no teaching methods at all, the new players will not know how to play! I am here to tell you that it is possible to both educate new players and engage experienced players at the same time through a combination of good design and basic understanding of human educational, motivational, and cognitive psychologies. Don't be scared; I'm going to make sure you get it with as little pain as possible.

This brings me back to the "tutorial." We are always looking to make our games more fun, but often times, we are not exactly sure how to do that. Ironically, while many of us think of tutorials in video games with a bitter taste in our mouths, the tutorial is perhaps one of the most important pathways to player enjoyment and engagement. This may seem hard to believe, given how uncannily atrocious players often tell us they are, and how oft reviled they are by games journalists and professionals alike. This very rejection of the tutorial, however, should tell us as designers that this is an opportunity for our trade to grow. This book is dedicated to helping game designers make sense of years of research in game studies, education, psychology, human-computer interaction, user interface and experience, and games user research in order to make dynamite tutorials that help their players enjoy their games. The takeaway from the book is a list of easy-to-implement changes that can make a huge difference in how players receive your games, which can be located in Chapter 8 if you are particularly impatient. I hope you will take the time to read through, though, and see that a little learning can go a long way to helping your players have a great time.

Video Game Tutorials

The introductory chapter intends to demonstrate tutorials to the player, starting with discussion of the first-ever tutorials in games like *Half-Life* and drawing on where these came from. Early tutorials consisted primarily of instruction booklets, as older systems lacked the power to display much on the screen. As our devices have changed, so have our methods of learning, and newer tutorials often use special "tutorial levels" or pop-ups to teach players how to play the game. Unfortunately, these are outdated teaching methods, and these sorts of behavioral techniques are drastically different from what modern learners expect or require. This chapter addresses what tutorials are, where they came from, where they are going, and why people think they suck.

Imagine, if you can, the very first time you ever played a game. Not a video game, but a game of any kind. For me, my earliest memories of playing games are of the sort of *Pac-Man* on Atari with my dad, who would die a few years later. Now that I think of it, it was probably *Ms. Pac-Man*™ because I played that one recently and the memories came rushing back. While this seems like a bit of a sob story, what's important to me is not the memory of playing with someone who I lost, but the imprint that it left on me. Just like this game, every other game I would ever pick up had one thing in common: I had to learn how to play. In the early days of playing *Ms. Pac-Man* as a 4-year-old with my dad, or *The Legend of Zelda*™ as a 5-year-old with my mom, I had capable adults there, familiar with my learning style, who cared deeply about me—and they were more than willing to instruct me in how to play the game. These were my first experiences with learning to play.

This guided experience wasn't always the case, however. It wasn't long before my mother had no idea how to hook up the *Super Nintendo*™, and would come to me to tinker with the plugs at 8 years old. I'd give her a handy beating in *Mortal Kombat*™ on the *Sega Genesis*, and she'd watch me blow through *Mega Man X*™ on the *Super Nintendo* or *Sonic the Hedgehog*™ on *Genesis*™ wondering how I kept track of all the fast-moving objects on the screen. Along the 4 years in the interim, I had moved from complete novice, unaware of the controls, how to hold the games, or load them into the system, how to even turn the machine on, to a complete expert. I had switched roles, at a very young age, from learner to teacher. I am sure many of you with children are familiar with this process. In a very short time, children are able to learn seemingly complex manipulations, like unlocking your *iPhone*™ and purchasing 11 copies of *Angry Birds*™ with your corporate credit card, for example.

Rambling aside, I grew up with video games. The important thing to note here is that somewhere between the novice and expert stages, learning occurred. Unguided by another human being, my brain overcame obstacles presented to me by a game system. This is something we strive for today in game design. We want our games to be challenging to the players to the degree that they are engaged, but not difficult to the point that they are frustrated. Even the most heinously difficult of games like *Super Meat Boy*™, *I wanna be the guy*™, or the *Contra*™ series prey on our sense of accomplishment. Because they are extremely difficult, we feel wholeheartedly triumphant when we are able to hone our skills to the degree that we overcome the obstacles that the game designers have presented to us as players. One could argue, however, that a game like *Contra* is simply "too hard." To that person I present a paradox. As many of us in the games industry are well aware, literally thousands of game prototypes are developed every year, and only a very small number of them end up as completed, published games. It only makes sense that many of these games are discarded as being either "too hard" or "too easy." One could imagine a laser-dodging game that is virtually impossible that quickly frustrates the player, or an "I win button" type game that provides no challenge. It stands to reason, then, that most of the games deemed "publishable" and, more importantly, many of the games enjoyed and commercially successful would fall on some midpoint of difficulty (see

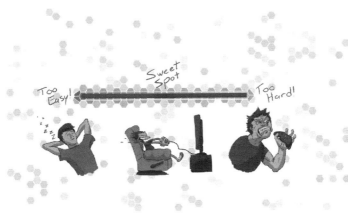

Figure 1.2 Sweet spot diagram. (Figure courtesy of Peter Kalmar.)

Figure 1.2), almost like an average in a bell curve, or the midpoint equation of a very odd game designer's caffeine-inspired scratch book (totally not taken from my notebook).

However, upon examining current commercially successful games we very quickly realize that this simply is not the case. Published games and indeed massively commercially successful games run the gamut in difficulty from extremely easy to incredibly difficult. On opposing ends of the spectrum are games like *Minecraft*™ and *Dark Souls*™, *Angry Birds* and *Metal Gear Rising: Revengeance*™, *Lego City Undercover*™ and *Call of Duty*™. This confounds our assumptions about games that are "too hard" or "too easy." The next logical step in our investigations of game difficulty should reveal a simple truth: there are different kinds of difficulties in games, sports, and life. Because there are different types of difficulties, it must logically follow that there are also different types of competencies. This is one element of our psychology that I will be exploring quite a bit in this book. One thing is constant: we as human beings seek an experience where our particular competencies are met with appropriate and associated difficulties (see Figure 1.3). Look at Figure 1.3 and think about the different kinds of competencies required to undertake all of these tasks.

So matched to those different types of difficulties are different types of competencies and, more importantly, different types of motivations. Some people are given to exploration, some to competition,

A Collage
of
Occupations

Figure 1.3 Multiple skill set diagram. (Figure courtesy of Peter Kalmar.)

and so on. We'll talk more about this later in Chapter 5. Let's think back once again to the early days of video games.

When the *Atari 2600* was the dominant console, numerous genres of video games were generally not available. People didn't have lengthy discussions about microtransactions, ARPGs vs. JRPGs, third- vs. first-person cameras, whether *Mass Effect 2*™ or *3*™ was truer to the fiction, or anything else so complex. It was enough that many bright lights flashed on a screen, there was a goal, an obstacle, and some way—with skill—players could achieve it. Even in those limited days of 4 KB memory stores and one-button controls, many different games with very different kinds of challenges emerged. This should lead a logical person to reject another assumption I often run into when teaching game design: games have gotten so much more complicated that they are harder to learn. I assure you that this is not the case. While it may seem like *World of Warcraft*™ would be harder to pick up than *Pac-Man* due to the sheer amount of content, I can tell you that teaching and motivation management are more important than anything in getting people to absorb the subject matter required to play your game. In fact, I am so sure of this that in my Ph.D. research I managed to get a whole host of people who had never before played a video game of any kind actively playing *World of Warcraft*, and playing it well! One of the major problems that leads to this conception is something called *element interactivity*, which we will talk about in Chapter 2. I promise you, teachers have been encountering and overcoming this obstacle for generations.

It is every game designer's dream to have their vision enjoyed by all kinds of people. Some of us give up, however. We think that perhaps, like beer, some people don't like particular types. Just like some people drink IPAs and others drink Stouts, some people play FPSs and some people play RPGs, and that's all there is to it. While it is true that people often form habits, and therefore rely on their pre-existing motivations to seek new experiences, the fact that they try new games at all is evidence that novelty-seeking behavior is still present, but not being accessed properly. Let me give a caveat: this isn't a book about marketing. I am not going to tell you how to get people to pick up your game, but rather, how to enjoy playing once they have. If your audience is indeed hesitant to try your game, you may have a slightly different problem, which I am probably not qualified to help you solve. Assuming you are able to get people to try the game in the first place, the way you are probably accustomed to keeping them playing is through rewards—fun stuff they are either given or get to do once they overcome game obstacles. This is actually a kind of teaching that we will discuss in Chapter 3, but for now, one of the best examples of this kind of teaching is found in *Heavy Rain*™.

When we let players die, lose lives, lose experience, that kind of thing, we are effectively punishing them for their bad behavior. We don't want them to be unable to overcome game obstacles, because then they'll never see the entire game we've put together for them. We don't want our children to eat glass because then they'll never live to see how awesome life is. So what do we do? We punish the players. Give them a game-over screen, take away some of their power, that kind of thing. We'll talk all about this in Chapter 3. For now, I'd like to say that truly great games wait until the player has learned the basics before punishing him or her. In *Heavy Rain* (see Figure 1.4), players start with innocuous tasks and on-screen instructions that show the users how to play before they are faced with more dire challenges.

Before anything gets set on fire or anyone dies in *Heavy Rain*, Ethan has to learn how to shave. If he screws up, the punishment isn't overly dire: he cuts himself slightly, and immediately gets to try again. This lets people learn how to play without making them throw the

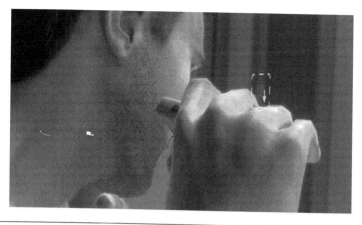

Figure 1.4 *Heavy Rain* screenshot. (*Heavy Rain* screenshot ©2009 Sony Computer Entertainment Europe. Heavy Rain is a registered trademark of Quantic Dream. Developed by Quantic Dream.)

controller out the window, which people will often do when they are frustrated or bored, which we will talk about in Chapter 4.

So, how do game designers try to get people to stick with their game? Oftentimes, it is very difficult to get an existing audience to migrate from the game they enjoy and to which they feel loyal to an entirely new franchise. If I were to make a new *Minecraft*, for example, I would likely not pull much of the franchise's fans away, no matter how good my version might be. Game designers are like any other people producing a product. We do a few things to make sure we are making quality products that will keep people entertained. First, we check on our competitors. Oftentimes, what other people are doing helps us to guide our own entry. Second, we check out what's popular. It is safer to ride a bubble, particularly for our first entry into the industry, than to forge an entirely new field (there are obviously notable and very successful exceptions to this: I'm looking at you, *Notch*). Finally, we start looking at studies done in other fields. Someone making a new movie theatre probably studied some food science at some point. Ever wonder why the popcorn is always fresh? Is it because the quality is better, or is it because the smell of cooking popcorn entices you to buy? Is the popcorn salty to enhance the taste, or to gently encourage you to buy that $9 soda? This brilliant realization prompted businesspeople to open psychology texts, engineers to learn carpentry, and salespeople to learn body language and interpersonal communication skills. After some looking, an industrious game designer is sure to hit up a local psych department's faculty publications and search "why do people play games?"

Answers to the Wrong Questions

At some point during their careers, game designers are going to come to the realization that somewhere, someone probably figured out why people do the things they do. A quick Googling on this topic will reveal all kinds of goodies, from Social Learning Theory to Motivational Psychology primers. The downside to this, however, is rather insidious. Oftentimes, well-intentioned designers, marketers, and researchers inadvertently worsen the problems they are trying to fix by bluntly applying the wrong research methodologies, assumptions, and testing methods to their audiences. The result is further befuddlement under the guise of improvement, worsening the problem.

Burton, Moore, and Magliaro,[*] for example, teach us that novices need strict worked examples in order to figure out how to accomplish new or unfamiliar tasks. However, Papert[†] and others tell us that people learn best by discovering things, making mistakes, and trying on their own to figure out the challenges in front of them. These things seem contradictory, so how do we know which kind of teaching we should employ in our games? The simple answer is *it depends*. This can be so complex, in fact, that many of the most cutting-edge game studios and publishers, like *Valve*,[‡] use multiple types of research methods to study their users' play habits in order to get the clearest picture possible. This kind of data triangulation is not only awesome, but as a researcher and educator, I would argue absolutely necessary to get any kind of picture about your players, what they want, and why they want it.

---

[*] Burton, J., Moore, D., & Magliaro, S. (1996). Behaviorism and instructional technology. In D. H. Jonassen (Ed.), *Handbook of research for educational communications and technology*. New York: MacMillan.

[†] Papert, S. (1993). Mindstorms: Children, computers, and powerful ideas. New York: Basic Books.

[‡] Ambinder, M. (2009). Valve's approach to playtesting: The application of empiricism. Game Developer's Conference, San Francisco, 2009.

The burgeoning field of Games User Research deals with the motivations, habits, emotions, and psychologies of players. This is by no means a new practice: companies have been applying "focus group" type tests of products for decades. Games User Research sets itself apart, however, in its interesting triangulation of data gathering and analysis methods. This new field is slowly helping designers and developers everywhere get answers to the right questions about their audiences, instead of the tired old methods and practices that ultimately teach us very little about our players.

Tutorial Levels Suck!

Let me start this section by saying you are absolutely right. Tutorial levels, as they currently exist, are forced exercises in futility. Like putting your cat in a room with a *Rubik's Cube*™ and shouting instructions at it, time is wasted, everyone is frustrated, and ultimately, nobody learns anything. In fact, I will be so bold as to say that the current incarnation of tutorials in video games is often worse than nothing. This is certainly brash, but the fact remains that just like the cat in the aforementioned scenario, the bitter taste in the mouth left by the forced labor will stay with you much longer than any incidental learning that occurs as a result of the exercise. Hatred of tutorial levels and instructions is oddly ingrained into the minds of gamers, as though we hate to learn, when really, we learn new skills every time we pick up the controller. Famously, *Far Cry 3: Blood Dragon*™ rather recently lampooned tutorials generally: "Press Enter to Demonstrate your Ability to Read."

Like the previous section, however, this is again an answer to the wrong question. Over the course of decades of evolution in game design, we have slowly started to include these abysmal, mandatory, unskippable, hateful tutorial levels that feel like having our teeth pulled by hot pokers. Consequently, we recoil from them and don't include anything at all. This is nearly as big a mistake as the tutorial level itself, and is a case of the pendulum swinging too far in the other direction.

If you picked this book up out of curiosity, wondering how anyone could be stupid enough to defend the tutorial level, I'm here to tell you once and for all: I am in no way defending tutorial levels as you currently understand them. You're right to assume they suck. They're terrible, awful things. The outcome of this book is to help you learn to teach your players how to understand the objectives and goals of your game, and accomplish them, in as natural, non-invasive, helpful, transparent, and ultimately fun a manner as possible.

Why Bother?

This is a legitimate question. As I stated previously, we've been given a silver platter of gamers who are already willing to buy the newest incarnation of our franchise at the drop of a hat, so indeed its a simple question of efficiency. Why would I put extra time into learning how my players think, and accommodating their learning needs in a game project that is already over-budget, over-time, and getting bloated with features? I can't fault you for this question, but let me offer you this insight from the games industry.

In the past 5 years alone, massive companies such as *Electronic Arts*™, *BioWare*™, and *Epic Games*™ have had major executive over-hauls, well-known game designers such as Tim Schaffer and Cliff Blesinzski have gone "indie," enormous companies like *Zynga*™ are reporting losses and closing doors, and the most inescapable fact of all, the core audience for current games is aging. Try as we may, none of us can outrun the inescapable grasp of time, and it is up to us to either mold a new generation of gamers to our craft or fall into obscurity. I'm here to propose that we can do this through basic teaching. In an excellent video called *Sequelitis*™, well-known Youtuber Egoraptor shows us how older games teach players by slowly and mechanically introducing them to new game play mechanics. He is actually discussing well-established theories of teaching and learning (see Figure 1.5). Let's take a look at how older games like *Contra* taught players to engage with the system in novel ways.

Look at Figure 1.5 and think about it for a moment. We'll talk more about this in Chapter 3, but the learning method in old games was very clear, and very behavioral, a term you will learn more about. When players do something we don't want, like stepping in range of a bullet, touching a bad guy, or falling down a hole, we punish them. Similarly, when they do something we do want them to do, like

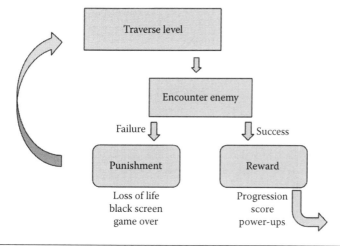

Figure 1.5 Old school game learning.

shooting a bad guy or clearing an obstacle, we reward them. This is the reason I brought up the dog training analogy earlier—old games taught in a way that wasn't really that different.

I hope that this will get you thinking about tutorials in a new way. Simply put, anything that teaches the player how to play the game in any way, shape, or form is a tutorial. Cast out your ideas of what a tutorial is now: an unskippable, sadistic exercise in torture that maniacally reads you the controls inch-by-inch, all the while hatefully aware that you are twisting and wringing your controller in agony, yearning only to blow the heads off some robot zombie pirates before dinner. I'd like you to realize that this is simply a very bad example of what a tutorial is. Making a player sit through an unskippable exercise like this is kind of like inserting a blank screen with narration at the beginning of a movie that says "YOU WILL GROW AS A PERSON AND BE EMOTIONALLY MOVED BY THIS FILM" and expecting it to work. The filmgoer is not engaged, not expecting to be spoon-fed, and not coming to this emotional realization willingly, and most of all, it is totally absurd to think this will teach the watcher anything! Beyond that, some games try to hide this blatant tutorial in a "starter mission," where for some reason, the badass super soldier you are controlling suddenly forgot how to aim his gun and walk. Barring a major traumatic brain injury, this is a dual sin of breaking engagement in the game while simultaneously failing to teach the player anything.

In the final chapter of this book, we'll introduce a hypothetical game as an exercise in design. The game is called *Escape from Skull Island*, and will play as an Action-RPG. I'll show you in detail how to use psychology and education studies to your advantage to make sure players stay engaged, and how you can use programming tricks to detect whether players are failing or not before bothering to jam instructions in their faces. I'll do my best to show you how to wrap good teaching right into the game's mechanics, so players aren't extrinsically aware that they are being taught. I hope that the outcome for you will be better games.

Cheat Sheet

At the end of each chapter of this book is a sort of glossary of terms. Many of the things to which I'm introducing you are psychologically and educationally heavy, and have a huge body of literature associated with them. For this reason, the cheat sheet will serve as a list of definitions of terms as they relate to game design. You can probably pull this portion out and staple it to your wall, if that works for you.

Element Interactivity: Element interactivity is a measure of how complex something is. Essentially, the more complex things a person has to focus on at one given moment, the more taxing it is on the brain. Something with low element interactivity is sitting on a bike, whereas something with high element interactivity is riding a bike. You must focus on more discrete things at a time to do the latter than the former. In games, the more element-interactive something is, the more time it will take to learn, generally.

Schema: Schemata (singular schema) are theoretical cognitive structures that dictate how we organize information in our minds. Players build schema around things like "guns," "RPGs," and "Consoles," and create meaning links between them. An RPG is a type of game, which is a type of interactive entertainment, and so on. Cognitivists postulate that this is how we learn and understand everything, and schemata need to be altered or adapted for people to learn.

2
THE TUTORIAL

Bolstered by examples in current games, the teaching methods demonstrated in Chapter 1 are illustrated as game design principles. Why did the designers choose to place the pop-ups in that particular spot? Why does game play stop when tutorials pop-up? In real teaching, how are people taught using tutorials? Where did the word *tutorial* come from? These questions are answered with in-game examples. Particularly, this chapter demonstrates with examples the three common types of tutorials that are found in contemporary games (pop-ups, special levels, and not at all), and explains them. It links them to methods of teaching that are used in modern education in a way that is nonthreatening and easy to understand.

What Is a Tutorial?

As I said before, you probably already have an idea about what a tutorial is. What I'm here to tell you is that idea is probably wrong. I'm not suggesting you are ignorant; what I'm suggesting is you have probably gotten used to sub-par tutorials. Just like you don't expect to be seated and offered a wine list at a greasy spoon diner, you don't expect a magnificent learning experience when playing a game. I'm also here to tell you that that doesn't have to be the case. As authors like James Paul Gee,[*] Kurt Squire,[†] and others[‡] will happily and readily tell you, great games already teach people things without trying. In fact, there is a whole community of scholars and game designers dedicated entirely to the purpose of designing games for teaching,

---

[*] Gee, J. (2007). What video games have to teach us about learning and literacy. New York: MacMillan.

[†] Squire, K. & Jenkins, H. (2003). Harnessing the power of games in education. *Insight*, 3(1).

[‡] Katrin Becker, Jennifer Jenson and Suzanne de Castell, Henry Jenkins, Eric Zimmerman, Katie Salen.

often referred to as the serious games or "Digital Games for Learning and Training" community. If you are interested, a quick Googling will reveal a dearth of literature on both.

This book, however, is not concerned with the litany of scholarship on serious and educational games. Rather, this book attempts to give you an overview of how people learn things, how you can teach people things, and why this matters to game design. To that end, the tutorial and teaching mechanics will be addressed throughout this book, but not in the exact way you think. First, we are going to get you to remove everything in your brain that even remotely sounds like the word "tutorial."

So, with that said, the following definition is the one with which we will work throughout this entire book:

A tutorial is any component of a digital game that is intended to teach someone how to play.

Whether that includes introductory levels, actual traditional "tutorials," on-screen instructions, narrations, mandatory levels, or something completely different is irrelevant to the definition. Even something as seemingly innocuous as incremental difficulty teaches players to play the game. Whenever we desire the player to learn a skill that is mandatory for overcoming the obstacles in our game, we are engaging in game tutorial design, or what I call *learning design*. I'm here to propose that game tutorial design is an intrinsic and inextricable portion of game design generally, and in my classes, I teach the two side-by-side. Expecting players to continue to play something about which they know nothing is hopeful, to say the least.

Why Tutorials Are Necessary

This is a very important topic. Many of my students react negatively when I tell them that they have to have some kind of tutorial in their games. This is largely because they are operating with the definition of a tutorial with which most people are familiar: an unskippable horrific experience through which we are forced before we are actually allowed to play. Consistent with education scholarship on playful learning, this doesn't have to be the case, which is what I hope to show you in this book. There are a few clear reasons why we have to have some kind of tutorial in our game.

Perhaps the first and most important reason is one of what you might call "high art" consideration: there is a fundamental disconnect between artist and observer. What do I mean by this? Well, when one looks at Edvard Munch's *The Scream*, it is up to interpretation exactly what the artist is attempting to say. It is widely believed that this particular painting is a demonstration of existential angst. We as game designers also like to paint messages and meaning within our games. This is one of the core principles that maintains games as art, and I am in no way suggesting we dilute this very important point. *Little Inferno*™, for example, makes one of the best critiques of modern disposable capitalism I think I have ever seen in any kind of media.

Unlike traditional art, like sculptures and paintings, games are a form of art that requires a skill set just to consume. Let me explain: in order to consume traditional art—say a painting—all it requires is observers to look at it with their eyes. Not much of a learning curve there. The second part of consuming traditional art is in observation: the trained observer detects bits of meaning and self-exploration in the piece. This is true of media that are more modern as well. We can't help but feel Charlotte's existential dizziness in *Lost in Translation*™ the harder we look. The break in consuming games is certainly not that our audience is not full of capable and learned observers, but rather those who enter the game-consumption game without prior knowledge don't even know how to consume. Kind of like if the *Mona Lisa* only looked like the picture we know when you looked at it at a certain angle. In order to get through an entire game, we need to quickly become proficient at its challenges to advance and progress. If we are unable to do this, we can't so much as consume the game, let alone get to the level of introspection that games can elicit in us. To this end, the first and most important reason we must integrate well-designed tutorials in our game is to facilitate the transfer of emotion, meaning, and enjoyment from game developer to game consumer.

The second reason we include teaching mechanics in our games is one that is a little more pragmatic: we want people to enjoy our games, and we know that when we have no idea what we're supposed to be doing, we aren't enjoying ourselves! If I handed you a puzzle, intended to confuse you, with no instructions as to the goal state, like a *Rubik's Cube* with no instructions as to what it is *supposed* to look like, what on Earth would you do? Maybe you would figure it out and start an emergent kind of goal for yourself. Maybe you would get frustrated and throw the cube into the Sun. One is good, one is bad, and it is unpredictable which you would do. Games that want us to figure things out for ourselves, for this reason, often have very thin mechanics. *Minecraft*, for example, has a simple interface and control scheme that encourages exploration. If I were to give you a complex game with no instructions, you would probably have to rely on existing schema to play the game. If you didn't have any, you would probably stop playing more likely than you would continue to be punished for not knowing how to play. Games do this all the time. Sadly, a lot of these are amazing games. Let me say that showing players the control scheme does not satisfy the learning requirements of your players. This is analogous to handing someone the controls for a commercial jet, giving them the manual that shows what each button and switch can do, then expecting them to know how to fly. Or, showing someone the notes on a piano and telling them to play Beethoven. Neither is going to happen, and for a complete novice, a loading screen that shows the controls for 8 seconds is equally useless.

Unfortunately, complex games often give us little more guidance than a brief introduction to the controls. Problematically, the vast majority of game developers are themselves gamers and they assume that their audience is already proficient and knowledgeable in everything they will need to complete the game, and even more problematically, they are often correct. These are otherwise amazing games, but lose novice players due to their approach. One example of a modern, amazing game with an absent or misguided tutorial and teaching scheme is *Amnesia: The Dark Descent*™. This is one of the more immersing horror games I have played in a long time. That said, however, the audience is clearly intended to be experienced gamers. How do I make this assertion? Well, the only tips provided in the game are "not to play the game to win," implying that this is what the audience often does. Furthermore, the game tells us "not to worry about when the game autosaves, or an autosave icon." A novice gamer doesn't even know what that is. This continues throughout the game: movements are available with no instruction and level guidance is minimal. One could argue that this fosters the feeling of hopelessness and loss that is common in the horror genre, but there are ways to do this without crippling a novice player. The clear counter argument is, "Why would I bother instructing a PC gamer that WASD moves people?" There is an even clearer answer to this argument: if ALT-F4 doesn't close the game (it doesn't), why should I assume that WASD makes me move? I will talk about some of these points later throughout the book, and culminate in examples in Chapter 8.

Finally, we create tutorials because the level of element interactivity (see Figure 2.1) of games has increased. We touched briefly on element interactivity and provided a definition in Chapter 1. Element interactivity is a concept that describes the number of simultaneous mental tasks to which a player must attend in order to accomplish the tasks in your game. In games like *Pong*™, element interactivity is very low—players must simply move up, move down, and block a ball with the intent to score. You could consider that three things to remember. In *World of Warcraft*, on the other hand, element interactivity is very high. This is because you must not only move the character in 3D space as opposed to 2D, you also have to think about levels, skills, statistics, items, item level, your role in the party, exploration, quests, chat, etc.

I would bet anything that no one has played *Pong* for more than 10,000 hours, but this does happen in games like *World of Warcraft*. Not only is this indicative of the level of complexity, but also the depth of the game, both of which require dedication and cognition. There

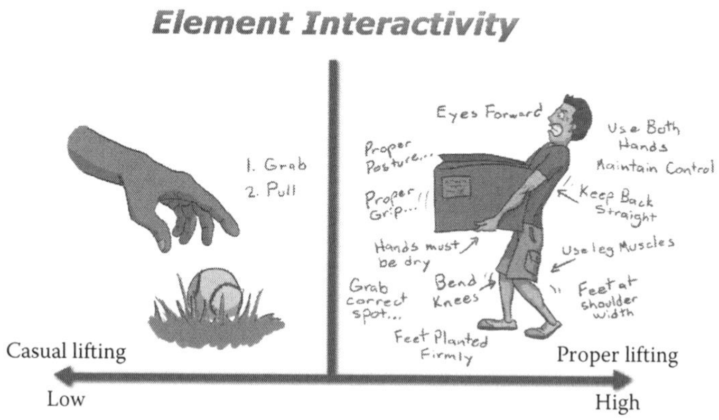

Element Interactivity

Figure 2.1 Element interactivity diagram. (Figure courtesy of Peter Kalmar.)

are other examples of activities like this outside of games. There is a difference between *walking* and *fitness walking*, between *dancing at a club* and *dancing in a ballroom*, between *lifting* and *proper lifting*, and so on. Similarly, you have to be thinking harder about the situation at hand in *World of Warcraft* than you do in *Pong*. You don't necessarily have to think faster, but your cognition is more occupied during raiding, questing, and managing your characters. Modern games follow a trend of increased element interactivity. *Doom*™ is less complex, mechanically, than, say, *Team Fortress 2*™. This is not a game value judgment, just a testament to the number of things one must remember at any given moment to be successful in the games' objectives. Increased element interactivity has lead to a steeper learning curve for modern game players entering the hobby than individuals entering in the era of the *Atari 2600* with its one button. For this reason, we teach our players incrementally, which I will talk about more in later chapters.

How Tutorials Teach

Whether they do so intentionally or otherwise, every tutorial of any kind that appears on a screen is employing some sort of instructional design strategy, which in turn is based on a learning theory. We will talk a little more about learning theories in Chapter 3. For this chapter, however, I am going to split tutorials along two teaching methods that I see in literally hundreds of games: *didactic* and *exploratory*. There are pros and cons to each of these methods, and they are discussed in the following section.

Didactic

Various dictionary definitions exist for this word, but the predominant meaning in education is that didactic teaching methods are designed as purely instructive, often excessively so, and in a way that is oblique, clear, and rigorous. Didactic teaching methods include drilling your times-tables, reading the instructions that come with your power drill, following assembly guidelines, doing paint-by-numbers, or following the instructions of a GPS. In a game, this includes following your objective marker on your minimap, responding to direct commands from NPCs or tutorial systems, showing information in flashcards, pop-ups in the form of heads-up display (HUD) instructions or hit point numbers, for example, or any other system that provides direct data to the player that is meant to be acted upon. Didactic instruction is very important for beginning or novice learners, demonstrated by something known as the *worked-example effect*. Without delving deep into the psychology, people learning new things demonstrate better performance on complex tasks when provided with a fully solved example problem. For example, if I were to show you the steps required to isolate X in the following equation like so:

$$\left(3x^2 + 4y\right)/2y = 3b$$

$$3x^2 + 4y = 3b \cdot 2y$$

$$3x^2 = \left(3b \cdot 2y\right) - 4y$$

$$3x = \sqrt{(3b \cdot 2y) - 4y}$$

$$x = \left(\sqrt{(3b \cdot 2y) - 4y}\right)/3$$

(Wow! That was way more steps than I intended!) you would be more likely to solve a similar problem successfully, barring any previous knowledge in the subject matter.[*] On the other hand, learners with prior knowledge of the subject often find this kind of teaching redundant, and it can actually damage their attention to the task.[†] Fortunately for us, games are great at detecting when you are having trouble, even via as rudimentary a system as counting the number of remaining lives.

Many games employ the didactic teaching method, such as *Red Faction: Armageddon*™, *Rogue Legacy*™, *Super Meat Boy*, the *Final Fantasy*™ series, *Spore*™, and more.

Exploratory

The opposite of didactic teaching, exploratory tutorials prompt the player to do something in a way that is non-threatening, and in which

---

[*] Sweller, J. (2006). The worked-example effect and human cognition. *Learning and Instruction*, 16(2).

[†] Kalyuga, S. et al. (2003). The expertise reversal effect. *Educational Psychologist*, 38(1).

they are not provided instruction. Interestingly, in education we often think of exploratory education as less "harsh" or instructive, and yet most of the more grueling games from the past used this method of teaching, with guidance, to teach us how to play. In exploratory teaching, learners are fully expected to experiment, fail, and learn from that failure. Obviously, this is not practical in some situations (e.g., nuclear engineering, airline piloting, surgery), but because the cost of failure in video game playing is low, games are well suited to exploratory teaching methods. Sometimes called "discovery learning," this type of education is as old as didactic methods, and is hotly debated in education and psychology literature.* In games, this involves mechanics like the "fog of war," by which players have to look and explore to learn, achievements that pop-up when you figure out controls yourself, emergent mechanics like those in *Scribblenauts*™ that prompt you to discover new things, or games that give you very little or hazy instruction while prompting you to wander and play around, like *Flower*™ or *Journey*™. On the other hand, this also includes hard-as-nails older games that were nonetheless successful despite their lack of (written) instructions, such as *Super Mario Bros.*, *Tetris*™, *Pac-Man*, *Contra*, and others. Players were expected to be motivated by the game's grueling difficulty, and learn to play by failing repeatedly through a kind of behavioristic learning that I will discuss more in Chapter 3.

In addition to deciding whether a didactic or exploratory teaching style should be presented, tutorials also have to decide when and how instructions are presented. In some games, like *Contra*, the answer is "not at all." Then again, in other games, instructions are constant and ever-present. Most tutorials are presented in what is called a context-relevant manner. Context-relevant refers to the context in the instruction. In the case of a teacher, I would discuss conjugating verbs in Japanese the first time you encounter a verb conjugation with which you are unfamiliar. In a video game, this might take the form of showing you the pop-up for swimming when you first enter water, or showing you the indicator that illustrates how many lives you have left

---

* Kirschner, P., Sweller, J., & Clark, R. (2006). Why minimal guidance during instruction does not work: An analysis of the failure of constructivist, discovery, problem-based, experiential, and inquiry-based teaching. *Educational Psychologist*, 41(2).

the first time you die. Problematically, context-relevant instructions do not take into account whether the player requires instruction. For example, someone playing a game like *Call of Duty* who has played other shooters probably does not need to be told how to reload, but someone playing it who has never played another shooter does require that kind of basic instruction. In real life, we would just ask people their background before providing instruction. Sadly, it is not practical for a game to do this, so in efficiently designed tutorials, we use programming hooks to keep track of when players are having trouble. We will talk more about that later. For now, let's take a look at a few tutorials appearing in commercially popular games and analyze their types of teaching, as well as when and how the tutorial assistance is available to players.

Three Tutorials in the Wild

This section will show you three common examples of video game tutorials you have no doubt encountered in your life. While there are all manner of tutorials out there, these three pop up most often. These are called *The Optional Tutorial Level, The Flashcards,* and *The Not at All.* I am going to take a moment to show you each one with examples, break them down into their instructional components, and, callously, tell you exactly why they are not accomplishing what they set out to do, which is, I hope, teach the player something. From the previous section, you have read that everything that intends to teach someone something relies on an instructional design strategy. There are literally thousands of these, many of which have been studied in great scientific rigor in the education community. To spare you the years of reading, I am going to boil them down for you in the following sections. Look at the following three tutorial types and their closest analogs in the education and psychology communities.

The Optional Tutorial Level

The optional tutorial level is something with which everyone should be familiar. These are the base creatures against which all tutorials are judged. The optional tutorial level is often boring, forced, and usually

Figure 2.2   *Rock Band* tutorial screenshot. (©2007 Harmonix Music Systems, Inc.)

slower-paced than the rest of the game. If this reminds you of being forced to learn your times-tables or fractions, or to memorize dates of battles you can't contextualize or remember, it should. In some games, the tutorial level is not presented to the player unless he or she goes looking for it, like in *Rock Band*™ (see Figure 2.2).

Problematically, players are often inexperienced enough that not only do they not realize that the tutorial level exists, they also have absolutely no idea how to find it, access it, or play it. For those players who already know how to play the game, this tutorial level is either a needless tack-on or a mandatory annoyance. Neither of these things sounds particularly good.

As far as instructional strategies go, the tutorial level varies. Mostly a didactic exercise, the level often spits instructions at the player in some way or another. Unfortunately, the optional tutorial level isn't so much an exercise in good instructional design, or evidence that the designers have taken a lot of time to get to know the psychologies of their players; rather, it is an excuse not to do these things. The assumption is that novice players will seek the tutorials, and experienced "core" players will simply ignore it. Sadly, it is therefore little more than an afterthought: a tack-on. Furthermore, the tutorial levels often get progressively worse or more absent as sequels in a series come out. Early *Guitar Hero*™ incarnations versus ones that are more recent are examples.

The Flashcard

Maybe more offensive than the tutorial, the flashcard is an absolute failure of good teaching that is unfortunately present in many games. Trying to teach someone how to play a game with a flashcard is like trying to teach a doctor to perform brain surgery from a manual beside the patient's open skull. In education, we know that many things do not translate well to what is often called "skill and drill." In some cases, straight memory is all that is required to learn something. This works great with things like multiplication tables, chemical formulae, grammar rules, and the like. However, it does not work for topics that are more complex, such as language nuance, interpretation of medical symptoms, engineering for bridges, and so on. Unfortunately, games often use flashcards that pop up on the screen to teach players complex information. Realistically, the only thing that should ever appear on a flashcard in a game is the control scheme. The instructional strategy is didactic in that it spits information at the player with the hope that he or she will absorb it, but does not verify that any learning has taken place. If the player fails and dies, loses the race, gets lost, whatever the case may be, up comes the flashcard again, equally ineffective, and now even more frustrating. Older games used positive outcomes with clever psychological reinforcers, such as flashing lights and sounds, to clever ends. We will talk about this more in Chapter 3, which is entirely devoted to how people absorb information.

"Flashcards are often used to study memory-intensive subjects within a defined curriculum such as languages, math, science, medicine, law, and so on."* In some cases, a pair of students will write the answer on one side of a flashcard and the problem on the other. I employed these when studying the Japanese language to help me "skill and drill" the characters and syllabary into my mind. Unfortunately for game players, manipulating the controller is a skill that requires more than rote memory. The exact mechanics of using a controller are a complex interplay of schema and memory that we will talk about in Chapter 3. For now, a pop-up just doesn't cut it (see Figure 2.3).

---

* White, M. (2012). Designing tutorial modalities and strategies for digital games: Lessons from education. *International Journal of Game Based Learning*, 2(2), 13–14.

Figure 2.3   *Red Faction Armageddon* pop-up screenshot. (*Red Faction Armageddon* Screenshot courtesy of Nordic Games.)

Sadly, this is easily the most common method of "teaching" players to interact with the game. Look at *Red Faction: Armageddon* in Figure 2.3.

The Not at All

"Good tutorials are essential for new gamers,"* however, game developers have recently begun to leave tutorials out of many titles altogether, like *Bayonetta*™, where players are literally dropped into combat when the game begins with little to no recognizable instruction. Part of the reason for this may stem from our extremely educated and game-friendly audience leading developers to the assumption that players have already played other games in the same genre. Gamers are often assumed to have built experiences around particular genres; often, it is enough to refer to "RPG," "shooter," and so on in order to recall the relevant skills, expertise, and strategies long-term gamers have built over years of experience. As I have already mentioned, raw discovery learning has been illustrated to be problematic for novice learners, so what does that mean for players of the "Not at All" type games? Well, often they will simply put the controller down in

---

* Hayes, E. (2005). Women, video games, and learning: Beyond stereotypes. *TechTrends*, 49(23–38), p. 27.

frustration, sort of like trying to get a 6-year-old to do calculus—it's just not going to happen.

Let's take a look at some tutorial levels from published games, and talk about what is wrong and why. Then I will link it to education topics, so you can get an idea of how this could have been done better, and how you should implement teaching practices in your games. We will get into much more detail about this later in the book.

Examples of Existing Tutorials in Current Games

This section will go through some current tutorials in commercially available games. Please bear in mind that these are all awesome games. I am making no value judgment about the quality of the games, just illustrating a few points about how the games teach, or fail to, and indicating where in the book we are going to work on those points.

BEYOND: Two Souls™

Games like this are story driven and, as such, the tutorial mechanic is light. I have previously written about the tutorials in games like *Heavy Rain* as being awesome, intuitive, and amazing, whether the developer intended this or not. Unfortunately for *BEYOND*, the tutorials return to traditional, didactic pop-ups. The tutorials are visually thin, which is great, because as I am going to discuss in Chapter 3, too much visual load can overwhelm players and make them forget, or at the very least, not pay attention to the tutorials. Unfortunately, no audio cues are used, and the game action is sometimes paused to show tutorials. Interrupting the action is usually a bad idea.

> **Right:** Tutorials are visually thin, appear in-line with game action.
> **Wrong:** Learning is visual only and presented with the same old pop-ups you have come to expect. Action is paused to deliver educational content.

Amnesia: The Dark Descent™

This is an awesome game, but thin in terms of actual teaching and objectives for learners. The downside here is that in an attempt to make players feel confused, frustrated, or alienated in accordance with the game's horror theme, the designers alienate new players by providing almost nothing. The game opens with a handful of tips designed to teach "gamers" how to play the game. These tutorial tips also reify an unfortunate trend of making assumptions about the audience; the tips are specifically geared to gamers. They are presented in an unskippable cascade of white text against a dark background before the game can start. Unfortunately, this is where it ends in terms of tutorials. Other "hints" that are presented throughout the game are the standard pop-ups you would expect.

> *Right:* Early-on learning.
> *Wrong:* Mistaking lack of guidance in an attempt to drive a theme with lack of guidance altogether. Great game, but alienates novice players. Tutorials make wide assumptions about player base.

Hitman: Absolution™

A rare gem of a tutorial, *Hitman: Absolution* runs players through a tutorial level at the very beginning of the game, before challenges are presented to the player. Unlike many other commercially available games, the tutorials are entirely sound-driven. This may not seem like much at this point in the book, but you'll later learn how the brain processes sound differently than images, and why this can enhance learning, particularly in novice players. In Chapter 6, I will particularly discuss how audio cues are processed differently by the human mind than visual cues, and why you should capitalize on this in your game.

> *Right:* Auditory cues deepen learning. Learning happens early on.
> *Wrong:* Learning is mandatory and unskippable. Tutorial instructions do not attempt to determine the player's skill level before providing instructions.

Dark Souls™

For a game that prides itself on punishing difficulty, one should not expect too much handholding. That is exactly what is included in *Dark Souls*: a barebones, pop-up-based tutorial that illustrates what buttons do. The game then drops you into combat with a big unholy doom beast from beyond the Sun. If you manage to live, you have effectively mastered the controls to a degree that you can attempt the challenges of the rest of the game. *Dark Souls* is hard. Unfortunately, it doesn't provide much learning to mitigate some of the difficulty and make the challenges seem possible. Further, it provides no guidance as to which direction (as in North, South, East, or West) is hard, easy, and so on. As a result, avid players will turn to wikis and online guides, while novice players will simply turn the game off.

> *Right:* Early tutorial level has clear goals and objectives.
> *Wrong:* Everything else. Pop-ups only, no audio, no auditory cues, tutorial isn't particularly meaningful, can't skip tutorial level, and so on.

Metal Gear Solid Rising: Revengeance™

A mouthful of a title, this action game in the *Metal Gear*™ series is fast-paced, frenetic, and requires many inputs from the player in a very short amount of time. There is a combo and blocking system to master, special slow motion slice-and-dice mechanics, and more. Fortunately, the game pairs on-screen traditional pop-ups that unfortunately do little to help players with auditory tips from the commander to help the player navigate the game's obstacles. One irking complaint is that the text and audio are redundant in that the player not only is told the tips audibly, but also a visual subtitle is present at the bottom of the screen. Arising as a limitation in voice-over quality in the early era of sound in games, the subtitles helped players overcome what might be choppy audio. Today, this habit lingers in games for reasons I don't entirely understand. There are no English subtitles when I go to see an English film; why are there English subtitles when I play an English game? Certainly, these should be an option for the hearing impaired, but for the rest of us, the result is negatively increased cognitive load, which I will talk about in Chapter 6.

> *Right:* Tutorials are in audio form and are contextually relevant to on-screen events and actions. The player learns both by listening and by looking, promoting active engagement in the game's tasks.

Wrong: Audio is accompanied with irrelevant, redundant sub-titles. The player has to visually attend to the tutorials while simultaneously visually attending to enemy attacks, health bars, and more. The tutorials are not always "on time," and you may be killed before you get to the point in the commander's speech where he tells you something useful.

Dishonored™

Dishonored starts like any other game of its kind, with how-to-move controls and pop-ups, and not much guidance. After figuring out basic movements, you are able to follow an NPC around to your first spat of combat. Unfortunately, as soon as combat starts, the game pauses the action entirely and occupies the entire screen with a visual-only pop-up, containing a text box full of information and images that demonstrate the player attacking. While the accompaniment of images is nice, as I will discuss in Chapter 6, the visually redundant education, the lack of audio cues, and the removal of the player from the action is conducive to reduced engagement in the task. This is extremely common in games, and you will see a lot of it in this book alone.

Right: Tutorials are contextually relevant.
Wrong: Tutorials pause the game's action and only offer visual tips.

Madagascar 3™

This movie game is an excellent example of how to use audio to hold learner attention. I can't help but think that this is because the developers knew that the primary audience would be very young. The audio cues are great, and narration is present throughout the game for tips and tutorials. On the downside, however, the visual text is left on the screen as well as the audio. This is inefficient and bogs down player learning, as I will discuss in Chapter 6. Other than that, though, there are all kinds of things done right in this game. Character voices are used to narrate the tutorials in a way that seems relative to the movie, the audio cues are great, speech is casual and well enunciated, and tutorials are timely and relevant. There is, unfortunately, an unskip-pable tutorial portion.

Right: Tutorials are auditory in nature, and the visual informa-tion on screen is minimal. Tutorials are timely, relevant, and read to the player in character voices from the game and film.

Wrong: Redundant on-screen text and an unskippable tuto-rial portion.

I have gone over quite a few tutorials here and given them a kind of judgment. I want to again clarify that these judgments have nothing to do with the quality of the game. I am analyzing all of this from an educational and cognitive psychology background. In many of these cases, the teaching methods are not consistent with how the mind actually learns things. It is my hope that over the course of the book, you will have a better understanding of some of the psychology of learning, and how you can apply it to game design. Let's talk a little more about what makes these tutorials good or bad.

You've Said Right and Wrong: Why?

This is a complicated question. I have spent in and around 10 years as an educator, with much of that consisting of formal research in the areas of cognitive and educational psychology. These two branches of psychology deal with how the human mind assimilates and stores information. My particular branch of research deals with how people learn from video games, not necessarily how we can teach them using video games, but rather the things going on in the human mind while we are playing. I certainly can't claim to know everything, but in my opinion, games aren't analyzed in this way very often, and it brings a new set of eyes with which we can examine game design.

That said, over the years, cognitive psychologists and educators have dug out some salient points about what constitutes good and bad teaching and learning. It is a lot of heavy research, but it is my opinion that these things can be boiled down into game design prin-ciples. Much of my work has revolved around reading, writing, and researching the way our learning can affect our enjoyment of games.

To that end, when games demonstrate types of teaching that psychologists and educators have long since discarded as being ineffective, it is hard not to notice. The worst part about this is that many of these problems have a very easy fix. Visual-only teaching, for example, has been shown to be significantly less memorable, engaging, and useful than those instructional methods that combine both auditory and visual information simultaneously. I will discuss this in more detail in Chapter 6, but this should very quickly illustrate to you that many of the things we are doing need to change for the well-being of the next generation of game players.

Cheat Sheet

As we discussed in Chapter 1, the cheat sheet is a fixture of this book. This acts as a chapter summary that goes over all of the scary psych stuff we've discussed throughout. Again, this is meant to be clipped out or compiled together—put it on your office wall, make 1000 paper cranes and have a wish granted, fold it into a little hat, have fun with it.

Context Relevance: Context relevance refers to providing instruction that makes sense within a given situation. When climbing onto a boat, for example, giving you instructions about how to cook homemade churros is probably *context irrelevant*. On the other hand, telling you how to put on your life vest is probably *context relevant*. In games, this means that our instructions must match our mechanics.

Didactic: This is an educational term and it refers to instruction that is direct, informational, and traditional. It is often used as a dirty word today, due to its roots in more harsh, classical instruction. In games, this kind of tutoring is direct and data-only, like controls on the loading screen, or pop-ups telling the player what the buttons do.

Exploratory: Another educational term that is effectively the opposite of didactic, exploratory learning refers to those kinds of education that require the learner to go looking. Allowing players to make mistakes and learn from them in games like *Super Mario Bros.* or *Contra* could be considered an exploratory learning strategy.

Instructional Design Strategy: An instructional design strategy is a type of educational construct that dictates specific methods of teaching. Whether knowing it or not, all games employ one of these. The one most often applied is *stochastic* (read: random). There are a whole bunch of these, and you should definitely read all you can about them to decide which is best for your game.

Learning Theory: A learning theory is a cognitive psychology, cognitive science, or educational psychology construct that posits a particular way by which people learn things. What this means is that it offers constructs and mechanics to explain the workings of the human mind. Early work was entirely theoretical, but modern theories have been backed up with functional MRIs and blood flow studies. It is worth reading more about these, and there will be further reading in the Appendix.

3
LEARNING THINGS

A psychologically heavy chapter, Learning Things is devoted to teaching game developers all about how human beings take in new information and use it in their daily lives. Teaching and learning theories are linked back to game design and the tutorial is discussed as it relates to educational practice. This chapter is heavily annotated, as it is probably the most technically complex in the book. Developers will come away with a better understanding of educational and cognitive psychology and how it applies to game development.

The other half of teaching, demonstrated in Chapter 2, is learning. It is no use teaching someone if they do not want to learn—Dewey knew this in the 1940s, and it should be known to us now. As we saw in the previous chapters, Gee and others have pointed out that games have some special sauce that makes people want to learn, and this has been appropriated to amazing ends with serious games. More appropriate to the current topic, though, how can we use that special sauce to make a delicious tutorial that keeps people engaged with our game? In this chapter, we will learn how people store information in their minds, what makes people choose to learn some things over others, and how we can use good teaching in tutorials to make sure that people want to learn what we have to teach them about playing our games, which will translate into longer play, deeper engagement, and lasting fun. I will warn you; this is probably the heaviest chapter in the book. I will try my best to make it palatable, but there is some thick discussion of how the mind assimilates information in here, and some diagrams that might not make sense at first. I'm going to explain them as they come, and there is a cheat sheet at the end of the chapter—as always—that will explain all of the terms we've gone over. Make notes so that you can refer back to them later. The chapter is also heavily annotated with citations of scholarly material you can seek out for further reading, if you are so inclined.

How People Learn Stuff

In order to understand how to make good tutorials for your play-ers, you should probably have some idea of how people learn things. Unfortunately, it is not as straightforward as a simple "how." There are a huge number of theories on how people assimilate new information into their minds. For the sake of argument and completion, I am going to show you a few of the most popular and well-supported theories[*] in an attempt to give you a holistic understanding of the human mind, and we'll get right to trying to understand them here in the text. I will show you some in-game examples, as well as some figures and diagrams to help you understand the more complex bits. Don't worry, it's painless.

Let's first talk about types of intelligence.[†] In psychology, we often refer to *crystallized* and *fluid* intelligence. Crystallized knowledge, or intelligence, is like long-term memory. Everything you have ever learned about a game, about the world, and about your favorite food is written into long-term memory and stored in schema. One's capacity to access and use this information is sometimes called crystallized or crystalline intelligence. On the other hand, fluid intelligence is com-posed of our logic, reasoning, and calculation skills. In games, we use both of these systems of intelligence, much like we do in our real lives. Unfortunately, current tutorials usually just address the crystal-lized knowledge directly, without having us perform any fluid tasks to make the long-term memory alterations needed to actually learn. In fact, the entire topic of learning is a complicated one that escapes most people. Teachers and educators are professionals who have honed the ability to help people to learn over many years; expecting to do this out of hand is kind of like expecting to open someone's chest and fix their pulmonary artery disease with a butter knife and no training. To that end, what is learning?[‡]

---

[*] There are a huge number of explanations of the structures of the mind. The ones I will go over are the most popular or the most scientifically well documented and studied.

[†] A popular topic, but originally from Cattell, R. B. (1971). *Abilities: Their structure, growth, and action.* Boston, MA: Houghton Mifflin.

[‡] An enormous question. Since this topic is insanely beyond the scope of this book, I'd recommend you start reading up on learning theories and follow the citation breadcrumbs back to classical literature from Vygotsky, Dewey, Bruner, and Skinner if this question interests you. The further reading section of the Appendix also lists a huge amount of classical education literature for your perusal.

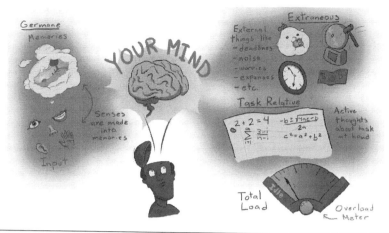

Figure 3.1 Cognitive load theory diagram. (Figure courtesy of Peter Kalmar.)

This will help me introduce our next topic, which is known as a learning theory.[*] A learning theory integrates the types of intelligences about which I have just spoken into instruction and learning. It posits different methods by which the brain adapts information and uses it, stores it as memory, solves problems, and more. Learning theories give rise to prescriptive instructional design strategies[†] like the ones we saw in the last chapter. Based on years of research as well as years of game design, I believe that there are a few learning theories that are of particular relevance to designing tutorials and instructions in games, and I use these in my teaching to help my students make better games. These are the Attentional Control Theory of Multimedia Learning,[‡] the Cognitive Theory of Multimedia Learning,[§] and Cognitive Load Theory.[¶] Of course, the downside of the numerous fields involved in researching human learning is that by the time I finish writing this book, I will have to add an extra chapter.

First, I would like to talk about cognitive load theory (see Figure 3.1). Cognitive load theory is a method of measuring the

---

[*] Ormrod, J. (2011). *Human learning*. Upper Saddle River, NJ: Prentice Hall Publishing.
[†] If you are curious about Instructional Design, check out the work of Mayer, Merrill, and Gagné, to name a few. There are a few citations in the Further Reading in the Appendix.
[‡] Mann, B. L. et al. (2002). Comparing auditory and textual presentations in a multimedia learning environment. *Journal of Computer Assisted Learning*, 18(3).
[§] Mayer, R. (2001). *Multimedia learning*. New York: Cambridge University Press.
[¶] Sweller, J. et al. (2011). *Cognitive load theory*. New York: Springer.

amount of load, as in processor load, on the human mind at any given moment. Under this theory, the brain has a finite number of resources that it can dedicate to extraneous, endogenous, and germane[*] load. Extraneous load refers to distractions, interruptions, and atmospheric concerns not related to the learning task, like bees swarming around your head while you try to write a poem. Endogenous is relative to the task because some things simply require more processing power than others do. Doing integral calculus, for example, takes a significantly larger amount of cognitive load than using the toilet due to its element interactivity, which we previously discussed. Finally, germane load is a "behind the scenes" type of brain activity that occurs as short-term memory is being stored in long-term[†] memory. If the additive total of these three types of load ever exceeds the player's maximum, he or she will enter into a state called cognitive overload,[‡] which we describe as being filled with blood-curdling rage and hurling the controller at the nearest wall, pet, or loved one. If you think about it, it is theoretically similar to doing calculus in a library (high endogenous + low extraneous), as it is to doing simple addition in a chainsaw factory (low endogenous + high extraneous). We only have so many cognitive resources available for allocation and if we use them all, we get frustrated and stop what we are doing unless our motivation[§] to continue is extremely high. It is safe to say that if a person is a novice gamer, he or she is not going to tolerate much frustration before quitting. After all, games are supposed to be fun.[¶]

Cognitive load, though, only refers to one part of what is currently understood to comprise human memory. Specifically, cognitive load theory tells us how the brain deals with our working memory, a component of our fluid intelligence that deals with processing things. There is another part of the memory, of course—our crystalline intelligence, or long-term memory. Long-term memory is the holy grail of

---

[*] Sweller, J. et al. (1998). Cognitive architecture and instructional design. *Educational Psychology Review*, 10(3).

[†] Baddeley, A. (1992). Working memory. *Science*, 31(255).

[‡] Mayer, R. E. & Moreno, R. (2003). Nine ways to reduce cognitive load in multimedia learning. *Educational Psychologist*, 38(1).

[§] Csikszentmihayli, M. (1990). *Flow: The psychology of optimal experience.* New York: Harper & Row.

[¶] Duh!

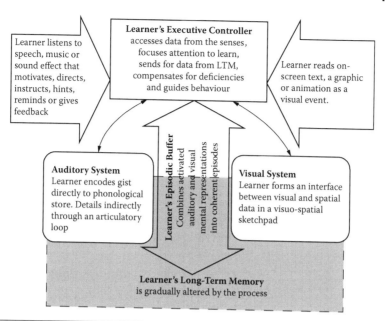

Figure 3.2 Attentional control theory diagram. (Figure reprinted with permission from Mann, B.L. [2005]. Making your own educational materials for the web. *International Journal of Instructional Technology and Distance Learning*, 10[2]).

teaching. If we can prove that we have altered someone's long-term memory, then we have actually taught someone something. How long-term memory alteration occurs is a matter of debate, but the two learning theories that I think best describe it in terms of games are the Attentional Control Theory and Cognitive Theory (see Figure 3.2) of multimedia learning, both of which share similarities to an earlier theory known as the Dual-Coding* theory. I will talk a little more about the key differences between these theories in Chapter 6, and of course, why any of that should matter to you.

Both the Cognitive Theory of Multimedia Learning and the Attentional Control Theory of Multimedia Learning break the human mind down into separate sensory components: ears and eyes, most particularly. Another theory by Wolfgang Schnotz is building on these theories with his *Integrated Model*, which also shows promise for learning from multimedia.† Long-term memory is gradually altered by

---

* Clark, J. M. & Paivio, A. (1991). Dual coding theory and education. *Educational Psychology Review*, 3(3).

† Schnotz, W. (2002). Towards an integrated view of learning from text and visual displays. *Educational Psychology Review*, 14(1).

using all of our available senses repeatedly. What is important about this in terms of games is that not only will single-fire flashcards not suffice in providing information to players, the fact that they are often presented in a visual-only fashion is absolutely not sufficient to promote learning. The Attentional Control Theory diagram in Figure 3.2 should illustrate some of these concepts more clearly. Think of the eyes on the right side and the ears on the left. The area in which you store information you have just seen or heard is known as your executive controller* and is referred to in the diagram.

If we think of the human brain as a computer for a moment, a few key portions are addressed in learning that we have discussed here. The first and perhaps most important is long-term memory, which is made up of crystallized intelligence in the form of schema. Long-term memory is kind of like a computer's hard disk drive. Then, of course, we have the RAM, which corresponds to short-term memory. We can hold about seven things in our short-term memory at any given moment, so we desperately need a RAM upgrade. We solve this RAM limitation by chunking things into groups that are smaller than 7 (see Figure 3.3).

What's interesting about our RAM-like working memory is that despite it having been tested repeatedly to be 7 ± 2 items,† putting in

Figure 3.3 Magic number diagram. (Figure courtesy of Peter Kalmar.)

---

* This is a component of Alan Baddeley's *Working Memory* theory.
† Miller, G. (1956). The magical number seven, plus or minus two: Some limits on our capacity for processing information. *Psychological Review*, 63.

multiple units of <7 items does not increase the net usage of memory. For example, I could remember, with very good reliability, a number whose composition is in <7 units of <7 each or, an order of magnitude easier, <5 units of <5. However, the corresponding number multiplied out is much more difficult to remember. Need an example? Try this.

$$568034092851298371259783$$

Close your eyes. How many of these numbers can you remember? Can you remember only the last five? What about the middle five?

$$92983\ 29123\ 19293\ 76956\ 12840\ 120394$$

How about now? Try the same thing.

Supposing you don't believe me (rude!), Miller did an experiment in the 1950s where people were able to spit back literally 40-digit-long binary strings without error by using similar chunking methodologies. This sort of thing is all over the world now. Think about credit card numbers, Social Security numbers, addresses (particularly if you live in Japan, where addresses take on a chunked grid-like number system), software serial numbers, and more. Our brains store information like this in a place called working memory, which is slowly but surely converted to long-term memory.

Returning to our computer metaphor, we also have our processor, which corresponds to our working memory and fluid intelligence. Our processing capacity is determined by something called cognitive load theory, as previously discussed, that supposes that there are limits to how much we can cognitively handle at any given moment. This area is categorized by our ability to process, solve problems, and crunch numbers and spatial coordinates. Our processors are supported by a sound card and a video card, which correspond to our phonological and visuospatial* processing centers, respectively. These are responsible for input to our working memory through both sound and visual/kinetic inputs. As I will discuss in Chapter 6, the brain handles sound in a special way, so stay tuned. Last but not least, we have inputs, which are our eyes, ears, nose, tongue, and hands. However, in this book, we are mostly concerned with our eyes, ears, and hands. Until the next generation of consoles allows us to taste our

---

* Also from Baddeley.

first-person shooter, this book covers it all. All of this is put together by something we will discuss in the next section, motivation, which is analogous to the computer's power supply. This probably doesn't make a lot of sense right now, so check out the figures and reread to really clarify things. The cheat sheet at the end of the chapter defines many of the terms used throughout.

Why People Choose to Learn Stuff

Mark Twain told us that work is whatever a body is obliged to do, and that play is anything that a body is not obliged to do. Unfortunately, when it comes to video games, things like grinding and repetitive play maintaining player attention sort of make that definition incorrect, and the answer becomes more complicated. Given that I teach people how to make video games, naturally I get many questions about games: why they motivate people, whether they are "art," whether they are harming children, and more. Often when I am teaching younger students, I have parents ask me two questions more than any others. The first is "Should Timmy be playing so many video games? When I was a boy…" which is a complicated question with a complicated answer, but generally the answer is "It's probably fine—at some point, someone somewhere thought baseball was a waste of time too!" This question is mostly included to demonstrate how frustrating it can be to give a concrete answer. The second question, and one that I think is more germane to this book, is "Why does little Betty love video games so much but hate school work? If I could get her to focus on reading with half as much intensity…" or some variant of this question.

A game does something that schoolwork can't: it reacts instantly to your individual level of skill. The levels get harder as you get better, and they get easier as you fail. There are games for everyone: some play *Angry Birds* while others play *Call of Duty*. The level of customization is astronomical. Games fit the needs of the player in the way a single teacher inundated with 20 to 30 (or more) students simply can't. Until we develop some kind of mechanical psychic cybersquid teacher, it is simply impossible to expect a human to know and react to your every want with instant gratifying feedback. To this end, I tell parents that it is not fair to compare education and games as opposite ends of a spectrum, because ideally, you are learning playfully at school and playing mindfully with video games. First, we come to games voluntarily; second, they are catered to our enjoyment, not fitting us to certain outcomes. When games move you, change you, or otherwise make you think differently about the world, it is through sheer art and skill, not through prescribed curriculum. It sounds like I'm really beating on education here, but I'm not. Standardized education serves an important goal for individuals, and of course for society, but it is simply not the same thing as a video game, so please discard your ideas of comparing them directly.

This brings me to the point of this section: motivation. Why people are motivated to do things is complicated, debated, and contentious, as most things dealing with cognitive structures of the human mind tend to be. While I am by no means going to tell you that I am 100% right about what I'm about to say, I hope it will provide you context within which to motivate your players. In order to begin with this thought, I am going to borrow from a man much smarter than I am—Professor John Dewey. Dewey was influential in education, and is still standard reading for people learning to teach. Dewey wrote prolifically, but the particular bit I want to touch on is how Dewey defines "experience."

> Through habits formed in intercourse of the world, we also in-habit the world. It becomes a home and the home is part of our every experience. [...] Yet apathy and torpor conceal this expressiveness by building a shell about objects. Familiarity induces indifference, prejudice blinds us; conceit looks through the wrong end of a telescope and minimizes the significance possessed by objects in favor of the alleged importance of the self.[*]

That's quite a mouthful. What Dewey is telling us is that our ordinary experience of the world is not the same as *having* an experience. As a somewhat orthogonal design point, we should be asking ourselves the tough philosophical and game design question "Are experience points in my game being earned for having experiences or gathering experience?"

Let me clarify this a bit: in the 1930s, Dewey understood that ordinary and regular experiences become codified by the brain. Sure, he

---

[*] Dewey's *Art and Experience*, p. 108.

didn't have functional MRIs, blood flow tests, and electroencephalographs to illustrate his point, but he was correct. When we examine the world, we automatize those portions whose details are uninteresting. They become uninteresting by becoming routine. For example, it is unlikely you are going to remember, if I ask you, what color the fifteenth house you pass along your route to work might be painted. On the other hand, if I send you to an amazing amusement park that you have been dying to see, you will remember your fifteenth ride.

According to Dewey, we enjoy assimilating information that we perceive to be novel. By creating non-ordinary, or might I say, extraordinary experiences, we solidify learning in the mind by creating motivation. This gives me an even clearer answer to the question asked by the parent earlier: your daughter is motivated to play games because the experiences are extraordinary. She is less motivated to perform scholastic tasks because the experiences are ordinary; that is to say, they have become repetitive and automatized. She is no longer motivated.

Now, Dewey would likely disagree with me, but motivation is described very well, in my opinion, by Skinner with something called *operant conditioning*. Skinner was also very influential in education, and is still studied, although his methods of teaching, often blanketed as behaviorism, have fallen somewhat out of vogue in favor of other theories that promote unguided learning through discovery, such as constructivism. While one might think that games are more like open worlds than behavioral training experiences, I'm here to show you through game design mechanics that this is simply not the case.

Behaviorism, specifically operant conditioning, provides for motivation in four ways, which I will demonstrate using the training of a dog to illustrate the point more clearly than decades of incinerated and electrocuted lab rats can. The four elements are positive reinforcement, negative reinforcement, punishment, and extinction.

Positive reinforcement is being rewarded for doing something. This is simple—give the dog a treat when he sits, or give your child praise when he or she does well in whatever hobby your progeny engages. *Negative reinforcement* is taking away previously existing restrictions. The dog gets to have a little more freedom when he doesn't poop in his kennel, then a little more when he doesn't poop in your shoes, and so on. Both of these things serve to reinforce a behavior. If either of these things happen within a few seconds of the behavior in question, it is likely that the player will continue that behavior. We accomplish this in games with juicy feedback, cool explosions, and neat things to look at and do. We also accomplish it by gradually releasing the restrictions we place on the player, like giving access to more islands in *Grand Theft Auto*™, or making you more badass in *World of Warcraft* as you level up. *Saints Row IV*™ is the master of negative reinforcement, which makes me think *Volition*™ has a talented psychologist on staff. The game places restrictions on your powers for a brief moment at the beginning of the game and then throws the doors open, which provides for nearly endless motivation and, of course, fun.

The other two elements, punishment and extinction, serve to remove behaviors. *Punishment* is obvious: the dog is yelled at when he eats your favorite shoe, or your child receives an "F" in French class for consistently making jokes about the pronunciation of "phoque." *Extinction* removes behaviors by failing to provide a reward in time. If you mow your neighbor's lawn while trimming your own and you are never thanked for it, over time you will stop. If you work your fingers to the bone on a special project and receive no recognition, you will eventually do the minimum required to complete future projects for the same employer. If the dog sits on command and receives no praise, the command loses its efficacy. Because extinction was discovered by providing no feedback, it is extremely important that you provide any feedback within about 3 seconds of a behavior occurring. If you consistently provide positive and negative reinforcement when players do a behavior, the result is motivation and a continued behavior. If you consistently provide extinction and punishment to players, the result is de-motivation and a discontinued behavior. However, sometimes players misinterpret your attempts to prune them, and instead just stop playing. "But Matthew," you ask, "how will I punish my players' bad behaviors, like falling down holes or shooting civilians in the face with bazookas, without risking de-motivation?" "Simple," I callously reply: you should start your punishments small, even reward them for failure, but your reinforcements should always be huge and amazing. Save the brutal, nightmarish, eldritch punishments for later. This fosters learning through scaffolding. *Heavy Rain* does a great job of this: when you fail early on, Ethan scratches himself with a razor—not much of a punishment, but enough that you know you have done something wrong. Screw up later, and Jayden ends up crushed to death in a compactor, wailing in agony while my wife and I scream at each other about how to get him out of the car. At any point in the game, however, the rewards are always awesome. You flick the controller slightly to the left, and it causes Ethan to be a badass architectural genius within the first few seconds of the game. Even at the end of the game, a few wiggled analog sticks and you are a kung fu master. The moral is, it is always a joy to succeed.

Behaviorism tells us a great deal about motivation in video games. As long as players are able to easily perform successful tasks, and those tasks are met with either positive or negative reinforcement, the result is lots of motivation! If the players can't figure out how to succeed quickly, and are instead met with tons of punishment or extinction, the result is very little motivation. Consequently, I present another key point of this book: it is of paramount importance that *all* players reach skilled play very quickly. If it means you have to sacrifice complexity or put in an auto-aim feature until players learn that they can turn it off, do it. The level playing field is one that makes us all motivated. It is no fun to play a game of football with one person on the team who has no idea what's going on. It is no fun to box with someone who has never boxed; essentially you are just beating someone up, you bully. This leads me to the last bit of why people are motivated—they are included.

Almost nothing feels as good, welcoming, and downright heart-warming as being included. I remember the first time I was actually picked for a team in gym class; my heart almost exploded. The idea that I was worthy, desirable, and capable released endorphins in my animal brain and provided positive reinforcement. On the other hand, being excluded feels horrible. When the two teams have to argue about who has to be stuck with you, the worthless bag of skin, you feel like human garbage. The question then becomes, why in the name of all that is holy would we ever want a game to be like that? Aren't they supposed to be fun? In my research, I have found through case study that many new players don't approach games like *League of Legends*™ or *Call of Duty* because the other players make them feel worthless when they are at the keys. This is called a club or clique behavior, and in fostering learning, is to be absolutely avoided. If your desire is to motivate and teach your players to play your game, you must not expose them to clique behaviors early on—they will balk. For this reason, clique behavior is a topic of significant research in mental health, nursing, and personal counseling scholarship.[*]

I have gone over quite a few ways through which people become motivated to learn things, or to do things generally. Learning new stuff feels good once we get it, but along the way, it tends to hurt quite a bit. The key is balancing our feedback through game design to make sure that players learn with plenty of feedback. This leads me to the next section.

How to Teach People Stuff

Gamers don't come to our games with instinctual knowledge of how to play. "Core" gamers, on the other hand, have a large body of knowledge upon which they can draw. So many of us grew up with incredibly popular games, we have never really thought about how people got into games in the first place. Well, games taught us many difficult things. I'm sure you don't believe me, but let's take a look at the very first level of the very first *Super Mario Bros.* game on the *Nintendo Entertainment System*™. This is a game I'm sure almost everyone reading this book has played at some point or another, so it makes a great point of reference.

For the sake of this discussion, let's assume that you've never played a game before, *ever.*

When you first start up *Super Mario Bros.*, assuming you're able to press the START button to start the game, you are faced with a little funny-looking Italian plumber ready to jump on things. He's not really doing much of anything, though; there's just music playing and we're not moving. Eventually, if your intention is to play the game, you will start to play with the controller in your hands. If not, you are going to sit there until time runs out, which hopefully will discourage your catatonia through punishment. When you press nothing, nothing happens. You are being discouraged from inaction through extinction. Essentially, you are being de-motivated to perform an undesired behavior.

---

[*] See, for example, Barton, S. A. et al. Dissolving clique behavior, in *Nursing Management* (2011). *32*(8).

Once you start pressing buttons, you are going to start figuring things out. The arrows on the D-Pad correspond to the movement of the player on the screen—one button jumps, the other doesn't seem to do anything. You will later figure out that these buttons make you run faster when held down, throw fireballs, and the like. You might say, "Matthew, you told us discovery learning doesn't work," and most of the time it doesn't. If you sit and wait at the start screen, you will see a demo of what Mario is capable of doing—he runs, jumps, collects things, and the like. This is called a worked example, which is a facet of the earlier discussed cognitive load theory. Essentially, seeing an expert do something provides a mental framework for you to follow. Alternatively, you could see it as an expert example, a facet of a teaching style known as cognitive apprenticeship. You imitate your mother when you learn to walk; you will try to imitate *Mario*™ with the controls. Each time you either make a mistake or do something correctly, the feedback maps right back to our discussion on operant conditioning. You are being reinforced to press the button and throw the fireball. It looks cool; it makes a sound. Just like a child's mobile hanging over his crib makes noises and lights when he plays with it, the noise and light is often enough to reinforce the behavior and provide motivation. If you need further evidence of this outside of the scholarly realm, look no farther than a slot machine or pachinko machine, whose flashing lights and popping sounds encourage coin-drop. Children's toys that do nothing but make noise date back as far as any of us can remember and continue to be popular.

Everything in *Super Mario Bros.* is brilliantly designed to motivate you to learn to play. Early on, your failures are not punished harshly—restarting the game is easy and fast and you can do it in a heartbeat if you die a million times without getting very far. There are warp zones to enable you to skip to a later level if you choose to work your way through. The "score" mechanic in *Super Mario Bros.* is virtually meaningless. Save for the *Nintendo World Championships*™, I can't remember a person who actually recorded their score in *Super Mario Bros.* However, it provides an amazing opportunity to motivate your players. The numbers are huge and ridiculous and clearly do not correlate to anything. They feel amazing to amass, though, and as you progress, you only get more and more of them.

When you make a serious mistake, you are met with death, which is not permanent, but subtracts from your count of lives, or chances. The teaching element in the mechanic isn't the death itself, but let's actively consider what happens when we die in *Super Mario Bros.* First, the inviting, jaunty theme is replaced with silence. The colorful world and interesting visuals are replaced with a barren black screen. Comparing the two side-by-side, the screen is positively festooned with color and graphics, and then is completely, totally black. The game is putting you in time-out for being bad. This is a clear example of punishment in the behavioral, educational sense. Not only that, but in true behavioral fashion, the act of dying is accompanied by a loud, cacophonous, sudden noise. The concept of pairing a noise with a consequence is not new. Dolphins and dogs are trained with a "clicker," and we too are trained, through punishment, that a harsh and jarring noise accompanies our death, and that we should avoid that. This dates back to the animal experiments of Ivan Pavlov, who found that often a sound is enough to elicit a response. He called this the conditioned reflex. Pavlov discovered that if he rang a bell, and then fed dogs steak, over time the dogs would salivate at the sound of the bell even in the absence of the steak. This would be a positive correlation, but we can similarly associate a negative correlation, such as shaking a can of pennies at the dog when he digs up your rose garden and salts the earth.

In the event you are able to continue executing positive behaviors, the rewards continue to be amazing. You get more coins and points, and this gives you extra lives, which are also paired with a sound that I am sure you remember and are hearing as you read this. The power of Pavlov's unintentional contributions to education scholarship cannot be understated. Good multimedia education, as I will further elucidate in Chapter 6, understands that your ears play a special and integral role in your learning. *Super Mario Bros.* continues to provide positive reinforcement for positive behaviors, such as the starman theme and invincibility for grabbing a star, the power-up noise and visual change for picking up a mushroom, and of course the ultimate culmination and ratification of our worth and skill—the castle.

Upon being able to continue performing positive behaviors and getting cool reinforcements throughout the level, you will be greeted with the most awesome explosion of juiciness that I remember in the 8-bit era (although there are plenty of other examples). *Mario* will jump up things that look strangely like stairs, inviting us to climb them. At the top, there is a flag, and you'll jump to it, or not. In either case, it will stop the music, play an awesome jingle, and then blast out fireworks (sometimes) and count down your remaining time with a ringing and jingling reminiscent of a jackpot on a slot machine with coins pouring out. This pattern continues for the rest of the game.

Super Mario Bros. teaches us to play by providing us with motivating conditioning that makes us learn the mechanics. The rewards are intrinsic to the game itself, and are borrowed right from the psychology of design. Minimal punishment and maximized juicy reinforcement serve to teach the player the mechanics needed to play the game. Bad behaviors are pruned out non-harshly early on, as the farther you get in the game, the more painful the consequence of death (you must repeat the levels you previously conquered to reach the area in which you met your demise). This is an important consideration, and later *Mario* games would refine this further by adding checkpoints and overworlds allowing you to save progress.

On the other side of positive teaching experiences are negative ones. I would like to highlight how demoralizing a negative experience with task-education (like learning to play a game or screw in a light bulb, use your imagination) can be. For better or worse, humans tend to internalize our faults. Even those of us who have an external locus of control, which means we tend to assume we have little control over our success or failure, tend to internalize and dehumanize ourselves at the point of failure. Consider this excerpt from *The Design of Everyday Things*:

> I have studied people making errors—sometimes serious ones—with mechanical devices, light switches and fuses, computer operating systems and word processors, even airplanes and nuclear power plants. Invariably people feel guilty and either try to hide the error or blame themselves for "stupidity" or "clumsiness." [...] I point out that the design is faulty and others make the same errors. Still, if the task appears simple or trivial, then people blame themselves.[*]

---

[*] Donald A. Norman (2002). *The Design of Everyday Things*, New York: Basic Books, pp. 34–35.

If we couple the fact that people tend to blame themselves for the failures they have in a system with the fact that people come to video games seeking enjoyment, their expectations are being violated by the system when they are met with consistent failure. This is an error in the design, and other novices would indeed make the same errors, as Norman observes. I would like to add my own expertise to the mix, and illustrate why people often blame themselves for errors. I conjecture that it has to do with mastery. The better we believe we are at something, the more likely we are to defend our certainty in that thing. Our belief that we are right, or can perform well, is sometimes called our self-efficacy. In game design, we often touch on this topic under another name—*agency*.

Let me bring this back to another educational topic, since by now you no doubt believe me to be a dyed-in-the-wool behaviorist. *Mario*™ has taught us well by pruning out bad behaviors, avoiding holes and the like. This is all well and good, but what about when we have a complex problem, or a problem that requires extrapolation of earlier learning? We know that in any platformer on the *NES*™, we only have a few buttons to work with. Up to this point in *Super Mario Bros.*, we've learned that we can run, jump, use power-ups, and that's about it. How, then, are we not taken completely by surprise when a platform falls, a new enemy appears, and so on? Like in education, repeated use of a task leads to deeper understanding. As a side note, and just like in education, some players just won't get it, which is why of course we must always offer learning support in the form of tutorials where necessary. Back to the example at hand, players are able to extrapolate their movements on the screen from earlier learning, providing it was rigorous, through something called *knowledge synthesis*, identified in a popular educational construct known as Bloom's Taxonomy* (see Figure 3.4).

Bloom's taxonomy is a tool that arranges educational objectives in order of their increasing complexity. Knowledge, Comprehension, and Application concern basic knowledge. We understand that the controller does something, and we can move the character with the controller to successful ends (e.g., completing the level). Analysis, Synthesis, and

---

* Bloom, B. et al. (1956). Taxonomy of educational objectives: The classification of educational goals. New York: Longmans, Green.

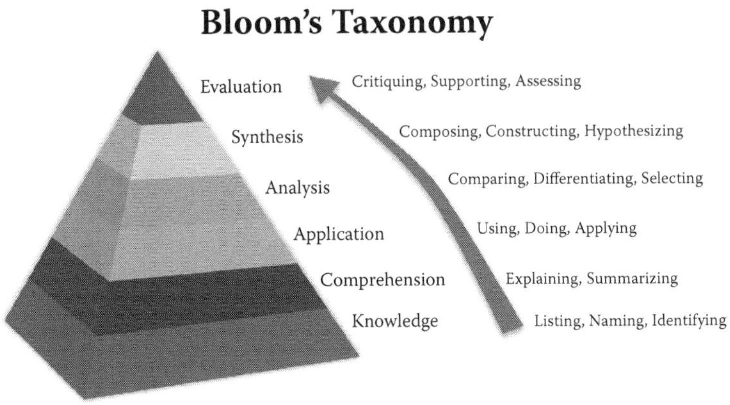

Bloom's Taxonomy

Evaluation — Critiquing, Supporting, Assessing

Synthesis — Composing, Constructing, Hypothesizing

Analysis — Comparing, Differentiating, Selecting

Application — Using, Doing, Applying

Comprehension — Explaining, Summarizing

Knowledge — Listing, Naming, Identifying

Figure 3.4 Bloom's taxonomy diagram. (Figure courtesy of Peter Kalmar.)

Evaluation, however, require a much deeper understanding of the content. This might involve understanding that one must jump and shoot fireballs simultaneously in order to live through a particular challenge. As we extrapolate knowledge we begin to experiment, and it is this process that allows us to transfer knowledge between games and across genres, which leads me back full circle to our currently educated audience, the dual-edged problem and blessing that leads us to the purpose of this book.

Well, that's it. While by no means an exhaustive list of all the cognitive theories of human learning, this chapter should give you a basic primer on educational theory from 1920 onward as it applies to game design. If you map educational outcomes to desired behaviors in games, the writing, teaching, and evaluations are strikingly similar.

Cheat Sheet

Following is the cheat sheet of important items from the chapter; their definitions are given as they apply to games. Feel free to snip it out.

Agency: Giving players control, or at least perceived control, over a system. The feeling of having an effect on a game world.

Attentional Control Theory: A theory that posits that human learning occurs gradually through a combination of auditory and visual inputs. Players use "gist" audio memory to aid them in visual recall.

Behaviorism: A school of thought that posits that all human knowledge is the result of learned behaviors. You do not touch the stove not because it is "hot," but because it is unpleasant. Strict behaviorists believe all human knowledge can be illustrated through stimuli and responses. Games and their teaching are often very deeply rooted in behaviorism.

Bloom's Taxonomy: A system for organizing learning outcomes. In games, this can be understood as a system for outlining how difficult the behaviors we desire from our players ought to be. Also provides for how learning objectives and behaviors become more and more complex as we learn more and more about a topic.

Clique Behavior/Club Behavior: Excluding players based on a perceived skill factor. Bill has to queue for hours because he is Level 1, but people who are Level 99 queue instantly. Usually undesirable.

Cognitive Load Theory: A model of the human mind that functions much like a computer. Humans have a limited amount of processing capacity, after which they will balk and disengage.

Cognitive Theory of Multimedia Learning: A similar but distinct theory to ACTML, Mayer's theory posits that learning is an active process in which the user must be wholly absorbed. Heavily modularized in the form of "principles."

Conditioned Reflex: Associating one thing with another through repeated use. The *one-up* sound makes us think of an extra life, and is easily used as a reinforcer. Think *clicker* training with dogs.

Crystallized Intelligence: Long-term memory stores about things. Facts, memories, and data. Games you have played and mechanics you have learned.

Dual Coding Theory: A theory that posits that information is best learned when auditory and visual information are used simultaneously.

Endogenous Cognitive Load: Mental load arising because of the complexity of the task. Because of element interactivity, things are often harder than other things; for example, calculus versus toilet use.

Executive Controller: Part of working memory theory, the executive controller is where all the "processing" happens in the human mind. Think of it as the processor that allows us to understand all of the things we take in with our senses.

External Locus of Control: A belief that outcomes in one's life are largely out of one's control. Bad things and good things happen because outside forces made them happen.

Extinction: Providing no response to a behavior with the intention of removing it. Walking into the wall does nothing.

Extraneous Cognitive Load: Mental load arising because of distractions such as music, flashy graphics, and physically external things like friends poking you in the eye.

Fluid Intelligence: Short-term and working memory capacity. Your ability to put memories to action, visualize, rationalize, and perform logic tasks. Twitch reactions and new mechanics you are learning.

Germane Cognitive Load: The background process load that your mind uses to turn new information into memories, schema, and long-term memory.

Long-Term Memory: Stuff we remember from long ago. Every game you have ever played, and every concept of genre, controls, and the like.

Magic Number: A psychological limit on the number of things to which a human being can simultaneously attend. Generally agreed to be 7 ± 2.

Negative Reinforcement: Removing something negative as a reward for doing something good. Complete missions, get access to previously inaccessible areas.

Operant Conditioning: A theory of learning based on adding punishment or reward (or removing either) in order to either reinforce or remove a behavior. Rewards and punishments in games are well documented.

Phonological Loop: The complementary but separate part of memory used to process audio. If I were to ask you to remember your favorite video game theme, this is the portion of memory you are using.

Positive Reinforcement: Giving someone a reward for doing something good. Collect 100 coins, get a free life.

Punishment: Adding something negative as a punishment for doing something bad. Walk into an enemy, lose health.

Self-Efficacy: Belief in one's ability to succeed. When players believe they can beat a level, they will perform the tasks contained therein with greater gusto.

Visuospatial Sketchpad: The portion of working memory devoted to visualizing things. If I asked you to picture a dog jumping through an open window, this is the portion of memory you are using.

Worked Example: A psychological effect that illustrates improved success in a task after someone has been shown a successful example. In games, this means showing players an AI performing a task before letting them do so, or illustrating what to do through level design.

Working Memory: A name for the part of your brain devoted to actively thinking about a task or solving a problem.

4
RAGE-QUIT

There are many theories about why people get frustrated, why they quit, and, in particular, why they react with venom to certain topics or even games. Ever hear someone flip out and say something like "Games are for losers."? That venom has a psychological root, and in this chapter, we'll find out what it is; more important than that, we'll figure out how to avoid it. Games User Researchers at numerous companies around the world are actively preventing rage-quits all the time, and I am going to share some of those secrets in the form of well-designed learning. You will learn in this chapter about boredom, frustration, and flow—what they are, and how to either elicit or avoid them in games via the tutorial system. There is some heavier psychological content here, so again, the chapter will end with a cheat sheet you can look at for definitions of the concepts explained within.

People stop and start activities all the time. These can be long-term activities, like that stint where you wanted to be a unicyclist, or short-term activities, like picking up a toy and playing with it a bit before putting it down. Why you start doing something is a matter of interest, and is beyond the scope of this book. What is important for people designing games, and in particular for people designing tutorials, is why people stop playing games. There are two reasons, and only two, why people stop doing something (being interrupted or having time constraints don't count); these are frustration and boredom. If your players existed in a hypothetical dream space where they had nothing to do but play your games, ideally they would never put them down.

Frustration and Boredom

Frustration and boredom are the bane of player attention. When players are either frustrated or bored, they disengage and start an activity that motivates them. Whether this is playing another game, checking

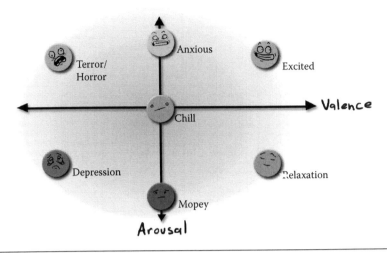

Figure 4.1   Valence and arousal diagram. (Figure courtesy of Peter Kalmar.)

their phone, going for a walk, or something else, the important part is, they are no longer playing your game. These two emotions are therefore very dangerous for game developers, and are mutually exclusive. Frustration[*] is what we call a high arousal emotion, and boredom[†] is a low arousal emotion. Valence and arousal[‡] (see Figure 4.1) are psychological concepts that represent a way to map emotions. Valence indicates the "positivity" of the emotion. For example, depression is a low valence emotion, and ecstasy is a high valence emotion. Arousal measures the level of what you might call "excitement." Think of it as the amount of brain activity that is happening. Something that is high valence, low arousal might be relaxation, whereas something that is low valence, high arousal might be terror. Frustration and boredom are both low valence, but are on opposite ends of the arousal spectrum, which makes them *theoretically* mutually exclusive.

When we design experiences for our players, we are dancing between these two extremes, buffered by valence. Arousal differs from game

---

[*] Ruederink, B. et al. (2013). Valence, arousal, and dominance in the EEG during game play. *International Journal of Autonomous and Adaptive Communication Systems*, 6(1).

[†] Van Tilburg, W. A. P. & Igou, E. R. (2012). On boredom: Lack of challenge and meaning as distinct boredom experiences. *Motivation and Emotion*, 36(2).

[‡] Cai, H. & Lin, Y. (2011). Modeling of operators emotion and task performance in a virtual driving environment. *International Journal of Human-Computer Studies*, 69(9).

to game. When we are playing *Minecraft* and joyfully exploring new terrain, this is low arousal but high valence. When we are frantically dodging bullets in a shoot 'em-up like *Ikaruga*™, we are high arousal and high valence. There are two ways, then, to keep people from becoming frustrated or bored: keep valence high or keep arousal right in the middle. Keeping arousal in the middle means peppering intense games like *Ikaruga* with breaks and power-ups to give players some time to breathe, or spicing up games like *Minecraft* with creepers and zombies. How do we teach players to have high valence all the time when they're playing? Tutorials. Tutorials embedded directly into the mechanics of the game, like the examples from *Contra* or *Super Mario Bros.* Let's consider a hypothetical player for a moment.

Going back to our previous example, when someone plays *Super Mario Bros.* for the first time, he or she is faced with a little dude that moves back and forth when you press the controller buttons. Valence starts low—he or she is just experimenting. It doesn't mean much to him or her yet, because the player hasn't created schema for playing games. As the player plays more and more, his or her long-term memory is altered, and the player gets a skill set that he or she uses to overcome in-game obstacles. The tutorial system of the game slowly ratchets up skill level by dynamically detecting failures and successes accordingly, not unlike a teacher educating his or her students. Skill is key to motivation, or interest, and was known in education classically to authors like John Dewey[*] and even as far back as Aristotle.[†] We therefore understand that as skill level in a task increases, there is a natural increase in motivation to continue performing the task. However, we also know that as skill level increases, so too do the challenges necessary to maintain a high level of valence, and therefore keep the player motivated. I would propose that this is one of the great challenges of both game design and education—keeping players and learners motivated and interested as their skill level increases, while simultaneously not alienating newcomers.

Let me expand on this point for a moment. Dewey believed that in order to be interested in a topic, we must have had an experience with it at some point that was positive. In other words, we are driven

---

[*] Dewey, J. (1913). *Interest and effort in education.* Boston, MA: Houghton Mifflin.
[†] Aristotle's *De Anima*, Book III, Chapter 10.

to further and further experience something as we are more and more able to see it to its end. This is easy to rationalize with common sense; the more marathons a runner does, it seems like, the more he or she tends to keep doing. To borrow directly from Dewey on this point:

> The gist of the psychology of interest may, accordingly, be stated as follows: An interest is primarily a form of self-expressive activity—that is, of growth that comes through acting upon nascent tendencies.*

This means that in order to foster interest, we must personally see growth from nascent activities. The "nascent" activity here in game design is of course picking up the controller and seeing something interesting happen on the device, on the screen, on the game board, or whatever you like. Once we see a personal trajectory of growth, increasing skill, and ability to perform more outcomes, interest is naturally developed. It is therefore the job of the tutorial to make certain that we are always learning, always growing, in order to foster continued interest in the game. This is not dissimilar from Aristotle, who told us that *it is the object of appetite which originates movement,†* which is to say that our desires (to play and learn, in this case) guide us to continue moving, presumably in-game. It is well documented that Aristotle was an active *Angry Birds* player.

Dewey also realized that artificially invoking motivation was likely impossible or, at the very least, extremely difficult. The concept of "making something interesting" was a difficult one for Dewey to understand. I'll relate this to my own teaching for a moment—my students often eventually stumble onto the topic of serious games; that is, games intended for a primary purpose other than amusement. Inevitably, my students attempt to create a serious game for an assignment or two, and often they do terribly. Why? Because students attempt to take subject matter first, and then apply interest second.

> I know of no more demoralizing doctrine—when taken literally—than the assertion [...] that **after** subject matter has been selected, **then** the teacher should make it interesting.‡

---

* *Interest and effort in education*, Chapter 2.

† *De Anima*, III (10). Classical literature of Aristotle, mmm, mmm game design!

‡ *Interest and effort in education*, Chapter 2. Your print version may vary in page number.

At this point you might be thinking

1. Dewey is a fatalist. (If we can't *make* things interesting, why bother?)
2. All teaching is inherently wrong/unmotivating.
3. How do I teach someone something without making him or her rage-quit?

Teachers struggle with these problems on a daily basis. How do I make the Kreb's cycle of acid oxidation interesting? Dewey and I would argue that this is exactly the wrong cognitive approach. I force my students to include a tutorial of some kind in all of their creations. Their answer is usually, "Aw crap, how are we gonna *make* a tutorial interesting/fun?" Again, this is exactly the wrong cognitive standpoint. Neither education nor the tutorial is intrinsically separate from the content to be delivered. It is not the teacher's job to somehow make the Kreb's cycle interesting. A teacher is not some kind of spice you can grind up into powder and sprinkle on bland food to improve its flavor. Wow, that's an *awful* metaphor!

No, it is a teacher's job to create problems, which the students must solve, that reveal something about the Kreb's cycle, and let the natural psychological process of interest do the rest. Game designers have a leg up on teachers, however. It seems like when a student has one bad experience being taught biology, they then associate it with biology instead of with the teacher, the class, etc. In games, however, it seems like players are more likely to call this a bad shooter and that a good shooter. Bad RPG, good RPG, and so on. So, take this as a message of hope, and consider yourself fortunate that you are not immediately slanted toward failure in designing new games due to the plethora of bad experiences your players have no doubt endured.

Let's take all of this talk about interest together, and consider a carpenter for a moment. While she has gained considerable skill in woodworking, this skill might not transfer to other seemingly similar skills. Place her in front of an arc welder, and suddenly the challenge is too high for the skill, and she is met with anxiety, fear, and ultimately disengages from the task. On the other hand, if you ask her to build a birdhouse, she is still likely to disengage because the skill required to do so is far below her level of experience. While at her job she might be forced to hang pictures, build simple shelves, or do things that do not internally motivate her, there is an external motivator: *her paycheck*. She derives her interest from the previous experiences upon which she has had a successful effect. She has built skill by altering her long-term memory over time. She has built confidence in her skills by continuing to perform positive outcomes at her job. Unlike a game player, however, she has that external motivation to keep working. Video games are something that our audience comes to willingly, and as such, the motivation must shift from external to internal in order to maintain our relationship with our players.

Again, this seems like a game design lecture, and that's the point. As I have said before, what you currently understand to be a tutorial is probably incorrect. Just as we often mistakenly understand education to be about taking a topic like moray eel spermatogenesis and somehow making it into an explosion of intellectual ecstasy, the tutorial system is equally misunderstood. Teaching works best when instruction and problem solving are key to the outcomes, not external motivators like detention (repeating a level), corporal punishment (loud noises, black screens, and controller vibrations), or stickers and bubble gum ("achievements"). Additionally, the tutorial works best when the mechanics themselves effectively *are* the tutorial and instruction is peppered in as needed. The carpenter will eventually burn out if her skills are not respected, students will drop out, and players will stop playing.

This all seems idealistic, you might be thinking. I've really only given you examples of platformers and shoot-'em-ups, which admittedly are mechanically thin compared to something like *Harvest Moon*™, *Kerbal Space Program*™, or *World of Warcraft*, which add layers upon layers of complexity into the mix. Due to the previously discussed principle of element interactivity, it is still possible to teach someone something very complex by breaking the mechanics down into smaller parts. Sometimes this results in a tendency, however, to insert wordy interjections in already text-heavy games like *World of Warcraft*. In order to minimize the cognitive overload we are skirting by doing something like this, we adapt our teaching method to be appropriate to the game in question. When I wrote my Ph.D. thesis, I used tutorials to help keep novice players both at a high level of valence and somewhere between low and high arousal. For example, playing *World of Warcraft*, when you first hop into water, you get a tutorial pop-up about swimming. The downside to this is that it doesn't bother to see if the player is having trouble swimming before introducing the help. In this way, if the player already knows how to swim, the tutorial negatively affects player valence, and increases arousal. If you were to tell the same carpenter from the previous example how to use a hammer, she would be insulted, in fact, irritated, which is a high arousal, low valence emotion. Why, then, does a system that is fully capable of detecting whether players are having trouble not promote optimal learning by offering tutorials at a time when they are needed? My argument would be that tutorials are a form of education, which is something people pursue years of study in performing. Therefore, tutorials are poorly understood. The designers know that they need to teach players somehow, but they are not sure how to go about it. The result is good intentions that sometimes damage learning.

Let's digest *World of Warcraft* for a moment. It is a very complex game to just sit down and play. Consequently, the mechanics need to be broken down bit-by-bit in order to correctly instruct the player, but how do we best do this? If players already know how to play, we are going to bore or insult them with tutorial break-ins; on the other hand, if they don't know how to play, we are going to frustrate them with complexity. The most frequent answer is to bury the option to disable the tutorials somewhere in the menu, but I would argue there is a much better way that helps players of all skill levels. This is where the explanations and discussions in this chapter come full circle. In education, two teaching methods that have been well studied give instructions at just the right time and remove instructions as they are no longer needed. These are known as *just-in-time instruction*[*] and *instructional scaffolding*,[†] both of which are part of a larger teaching and instructional method known as *cognitive apprenticeship*.[‡]

---

[*] Gee (2003) refers to just-in-time instruction in games, and a theory-heavy citation is Kester, L. et al. (2001). Just-in-time information presentation and the acquisition of complex cognitive skills. *Computers in Human Behavior*, 17(4).

[†] Tsai, F. H. et al. (2013). The importance and use of targeted content knowledge with scaffolding aid in educational simulation games. *Interactive Learning Environments*, 21(2).

[‡] Chang, W. C. et al. (2013). Game-based history ubiquitous learning environment through cognitive apprenticeship. *Information Technology Convergence*, 253.

Let's discuss those three terms. First, just-in-time instruction refers to instructions that are given at the precise moment when a learner is about to disengage, due to either frustration or boredom, which as we've discussed are the primary reasons people stop engaging in a task and, ultimately, stop learning. This is easy for an educator because an experienced teacher can see when his students are about to disengage and intervene. For example, if a student is performing a calculus task and getting frustrated, perhaps due to not remembering the appropriate formula, the teacher can become aware of this through years of training and practice in recognizing physiological signs of disengagement, such as crossed arms, certain facial expressions, lack of physical attentiveness, and so on. The teacher will then intervene with an instructional solution to keep the learner on task. This is, of course, not the same action taken by a game system. In fact, a game has to use programming hooks to detect when players perform certain behaviors, and then adapt procedurally to that behavior in order to either correct it or encourage it. In that regard, there is a certain behavioral element to just-in-time instruction, as we discussed in Chapter 3. Let's take a look at an example.

Referring back to *World of Warcraft*, the swimming pop-up illustrates how to swim even if the player already knows how (so long as the tutorial is turned on). Again, patronizing skilled players will result in them turning the tutorials off entirely, and potentially missing information they could use later, or simply frustrate them, lowering their valence and increasing their arousal. Now, what if the game instead detected when the player was having trouble, say, by drowning, a mechanic that is already present in *World of Warcraft*? Another example might be the hearthstone, which is an item in *World of Warcraft* that returns you to a chosen location. The hearthstone takes a few seconds to channel, and can be interrupted by moving, using another spell, or taking damage. The tutorial by default pops up when you first interact with the item. Why not wait to see if the players figure it out themselves and offer help only when the players fail to do so? This is significantly more consistent with how humans learn and accords nicely with just-in-time teaching. To boot, it is not that difficult: the simple code snippet below keeps track of player errors in using the hearthstone and interjects with a tutorial when it becomes necessary. If the players don't make mistakes, no tutorial pop-up. It is written in Lua, which is the language of *World of Warcraft* add-ons, but it should be easy to read:

```
--> Hearthstone Tutorial Tip (Just-In-Time)
if (event == "UNIT_SPELLCAST_INTERRUPTED") then
     local _,m,_ = ...
     --> "m" stores spell names. t[x] is an array
         storing tips.
     --> Triggers when casting is interrupted by
         moving, etc.
     if (m == "Hearthstone") then
          if not t[30] then
               tFail[30] = tFail[30] + 1
               if (tFail[30] > 3) then
               --> tFail keeps track of bad behaviors.
               --> if players interrupt the
                   hearthstone 3 times
                    JIT_Trigger(31)
                    t[30] = true
                    --> Run a function to show the
                        tutorial.
               end
          end
     end
end
```

On the other hand, we can also front-load our instruction and take it away when players start to do well. This is the exact inverse of just-in-time instruction, and is known as instructional scaffolding. Much like the scaffolds on a building, instruction is offered to give students access to the game, and then removed as they start to do better. Depending on the type of game and the desires of the designer, the well-designed tutorial might offer instruction off-the-bat, and then fade it away as players become more skilled, bringing it back when players make mistakes, in a sort of half scaffold, half just-in-time teaching method. This means writing programming hooks to detect both desirable and undesirable behaviors, and programming tutorials to intervene or fade away accordingly. This is helpful with very complex topics, such as attaching joints and mounting points in *Kerbal Space Program*. In a well-designed scaffolded tutorial, players

are assumed to never have used the system before, but if they succeed, the tutorials are quickly taken away. Let's take a look at some
pseudocode to write a scaffolded version of the hearthstone tutorial
modification illustrated previously. Admittedly, using the hearthstone
isn't the most complicated process in the world, but it will serve to
demonstrate a point and illustrate some pseudocode that I use to com-
municate with programmers on my projects.

```
//Pseudocode for Hearthstone (Scaffolded)
var tipIndex[60];
populateArray(tipIndex);
//assume array is full of relevant tips
//let tipIndex 31 = Hearthstone

function ShowHearthStoneTip(timeArg)
{
     showTip(31);
     timeOnScreen = timeArg;
     shownTip[31] = true;
}

if (shownTip(31) == true && HearthstoneInterrupted ==
true)
{
     tipIndex[31].failure ++;
}

//set a low failure threshold

if (tipIndex[31].failure >= 3)
{
     shownTip[31] = false;
}

function OnHearthStoneCast()
{
     if (shownTip[31] == false)
     {
          ShowHearthStoneTip(tipIndex[31].failure || 3.0);
     }
}
```

Unlike the previous example, this piece of instruction is front-
loaded. That is to say, it shows the tip right off the bat, assuming that

the player doesn't know what's going on. While this may not be the case, if the player doesn't fail at things, he or she will never see the tip again. On the other hand, the more the player fails, the more often (and longer) the player sees the tip. Like its namesake, instructional scaffolding refers to assistance in the building process. When scaffolding a building, we build parts that allow us access to higher levels without the actual building's structure being in place. In education, we offer help to students to reach higher or more difficult portions of the instruction. As the building is raised, the scaffolds are removed. In education, this means removing tips, tutorials, or pop-ups as the player or student gains mastery in the topic. When we blend instructional scaffolding with something known as *modeling*, mimicking the behavior of a master or adept, we come up with something known in education as *cognitive apprenticeship*.

Cognitive Apprenticeship

Cognitive apprenticeship is a method of teaching that borrows from traditional forms of apprenticeship; a master illustrates good form to his apprentices and students. Unlike in a traditional apprenticeship, however, cognitive masters lend some of their advanced schema to their students to lessen cognitive load. Let me explain further: suppose you have trouble with the quadratic equation. Someone who has expert-level knowledge in this area can demonstrate a problem to you, chunk the equation into smaller pieces, and then aid you through problems. They will gradually remove their assistance until your schema adapts to fit theirs. Thus, through a combination of modeling—imitating a master-level practitioner of a skill—and scaffolding, we form a kind of apprenticeship with our teachers. How does this relate to game design?

Numerous games give us expert players after which we must model our own behavior. Egoraptor* shows us how *Mega Man X* creates an apprenticeship relationship through the NPC *Zero*™, who is much stronger and more capable than the protagonist, creating a feeling of emulation and constant improvement. I would say, however, that the

---

* "Sequelitis: Mega Man X." Link at time of writing: http://www.youtube.com/user/egoraptor.

Figure 4.2   Screenshot from *UNCHARTED*. (UNCHARTED: Drake's Fortune screenshot ©2007 Sony Computer Entertainment America LLC. UNCHARTED: Drake's Fortune is a registered trademark of Sony Computer Entertainment America LLC. Created and developed by Naughty Dog, Inc.)

feeling of disempowerment is not always necessary for the apprentice. A perfect example of cognitive apprenticeship through tutorial design in games is presented in *UNCHARTED: Drake's Fortune*™ (see Figure 4.2). In the first game of the series, the first moment the player gains control is marked by a gunfight with pirates off the coast of Panama. Keeping with modern games, this isn't too far off from the norm; however, the player encounters the pirates with an AI partner, *Elena Pierce*™.

One of the mechanics necessary to be successful in *UNCHARTED*™ and many other shooters is cover. In a firefight, it's probably a good idea to get behind something and pray for your life. *UNCHARTED* double-dips by providing you with a pop-up about how to take cover, very briefly on the screen, and by illustrating mastery behavior through the AI, *Elena*™. I would argue that *Drake*™ is spun, in this particular story, to be the suave, debonair badass; however, *Elena* makes for cover almost immediately. For non-initiate players, this indicates very quickly that they need to emulate the behavior of the now cognitive master in order to stay alive and observe tips. By seeking cover, the players are able to avoid negative consequences (death), and return fire. In so doing, they complete objectives, feel like a badass, and are given rewards (more levels, story completion). It's this cycle that players become interested in the game, as we have already discussed. In true form, the instruction is scaffolded; the tips on the screen fade away, but the AI player present is a constant reminder of your cognitive apprenticeship. You are no longer given tips, but you are still given a master to model. In the most difficult parts of the game, *Drake* is forced to meet challenges alone, and this profound separation of character and AI companion only further drives home the game's theme of camaraderie and cooperation, while simultaneously ratcheting up the difficulty at just the right moment. If you needed any more reason why this game won dumpsters full of awards, here it is.

We've talked a lot about the things that make people throw controllers at the wall. Conversely, we've talked about a lot of the educational interventions that can keep people from doing things like that. Dewey let us know that interest is a factor of skill, and that increasing interest was a facet of receiving reinforcement in our performance, while simultaneously being met with new challenges. One last thing I would like to talk about in this chapter is one that comes up a lot in discussions of media, motivation, and particularly game design: flow.

"Flow" and Other Reasons People Keep Playing

A concept piloted by Mihalyi Csikszentmihayli, *flow* refers to the moment in our psychology when we are "in the zone" (see Figure 4.3). This occurs when our level of skill is perfectly met with an equal challenge. It is a psychological state characterized by uncharacteristic

Figure 4.3 Flow channel diagram. (Figure courtesy of Peter Kalmar.)

performance, single-minded focus, loss of temporal perception, and complete *ensorcellement* in the task at hand. More importantly, it feels freaking amazing. Flow is one of the many things that keep us playing games. While the causes of flow are complicated and far-reaching, the quintessential portion that we can harness in game design is that skill level and difficulty have to ratchet up simultaneously, both through good instruction and well-designed experiences to test that instruction. This is also true in education—students achieve a flow state when they are learning at an alarming rate of efficiency; each new tidbit of information is being met precisely with an appropriate challenge to their current schemata and skill levels.

Because we know that frustration and boredom stop people from playing, logically there must be an opposite end of the spectrum: the things that keep people playing. Flow is one such thing. *Flow* is a widely used buzzword often employed to describe more or less any focused amusement. When someone is engaged heavily in a task that they appear to be enjoying, oftentimes this will be referred to as flow. Factually, there are many ways to measure flow experiences, and there are studied and established metrics used to demonstrate whether the psychological state actually emerged, or if the players were simply distracted. I am certainly not saying flow doesn't happen in games by any means. A plethora of studies have illustrated through scientifically rigorous means that flow is definitely happening.[*] What I am suggesting is a general increase in rigor in determining whether something genuinely constitutes a flow state. There are instruments available to measure flow experiences, such as the DFS-2, which has been evaluated against game experiences on numerous occasions.[†] Suffice to say, even these scales and tests often become the subject of license fees and more. It is paradoxically difficult to measure flow physiologically, as the things that would measure flow would also discourage it; for example, sticking a person's face full of electromyographic electrodes. As a boil down, a flow state is indicated if many of the following things are observable in the player:

---

[*] Procci, K. et al. (2013). Measuring the flow experience of gamers: An evaluation of the DFS-2. *Computers in Human Behavior*, 28(6).

[†] Wang, C. K. J., Liu, W. C., & Khoo, A. (2009). The psychometric properties of dispositional flow-scale 2 in internet gaming. *Current Psychology*, 28.

- **Perfect balance between challenge and skill.** Player is accomplishing tasks, but using all of his or her energy to do so.
- **Loss of self.** Player becomes unaware of surroundings.
- **Autotelism.** Only observable in interview post-activity, player seems to want to continue activity for no reason other than the intrinsic value of the activity itself.
- **Temporal distortion.** Player becomes unaware of passage of time.
- **Clear feedback.** Player is able to relay the success/failure of his or her performance with perfect clarity.
- **Loss of awareness.** Player reports a feeling of acting by magic or automation to meet tasks and challenges.
- **High self-efficacy.** Player feels capable of meeting tasks assigned to him or her.
- **Clear goals and outcomes.** Player states he or she knew exactly how to achieve goals/outcomes.

Because flow is awesome, we want to encourage it in our game design. Because flow is rooted in psychology, educators are able to manipulate and change their teaching styles in such a way as to bring it about. Following that logic, game designers can teach their players to play their games in such a way as to bring about flow experiences in games. There are three points in the flow experience checklist provided above that are particularly notable to the tutorial and teaching design of the game: *balance* between challenge and skill, *feedback*, and *clarity* of goals and outcomes. Each of these relate to how players have been taught to play the game: their skills need to improve along with the challenges in order to match properly, they must be given regular and clear feedback, and there must be clarity in purpose.

Balance

The first component of flow I will elucidate with reference to the game's teaching mechanics is balance of skill and challenge. In some of the code demonstrated earlier, I made it clear that it is possible to detect when players are having trouble in a game. In the examples given, players were unable to properly cast a spell, unable to properly swim, and so on. In education, we use tests like these to verify that learning has occurred; on the other hand, when students fail the tests, we know that it hasn't. In order to promote flow experiences in games, we need to make sure that all players arrive at the same skill level as fast as possible. What this means is that tutorials must illustrate the points of the game to the player rapidly, whether through pop-ups, cognitive apprenticeship modeling, or some other method. We realize the importance of having a skill-challenge balance in eliciting flow. In Chapter 3, we learned how to teach people particular things in games, and how we should introduce additional challenges to extrapolate from prior learning. If this is happening successfully, challenge and skill level will be in perfect balance. The clearest way to promote good behaviors and cull out bad ones in order to reach this balance is through consistent and constant *feedback*.

Feedback

A second hallmark of flow illustrated in the flow scale described previously is the presence of clear and unambiguous feedback. While I could write an entire book on the feedback loop in video games, I will demonstrate with a few key examples. Both *Contra* and *Super Mario Bros.* as previously described use feedback to either reinforce or discourage particular behaviors in games. Tens of thousands of individuals studied experiencing flow have universally relayed the fact that they were exactly aware of how well or poorly they were doing at any given moment. For this reason, it is very important to punish failure and reward success harshly, quickly, and overtly. While this may not be the case at the very beginning of the game, where we are trying to reward experimentation and innovation in order to "grow from a nascent experience," we do want to ramp up the punishments for failure significantly, and ensure that the rewards for success are always amazing. Finally, players must always know how to reach success or failure, and what behaviors will bring them to a successful or failed state in order to maintain *clear outcomes*.

Clear Outcomes

In years of flow study, one additional facet that recurs consistently is that individuals studied were exactly aware of what was required of them in order to succeed, and what behaviors would lead them to failure. Consistent with having a high skill level, flow-experienced players will be able to relay behaviors that will lead to death ("don't fall down there, you'll die"), and behaviors that will lead to pleasant feedback ("jump as high as you can to get the best score!"). Let me digress for a moment: in my years in university, one particularly inspirational professor gave three students and me each a golf club. He brought us to the front of the class, golf clubs in hand, and placed three balls on the floor. He said to hit them in any way we liked. Since we were indoors, we all invariably putted our golf balls across the room in different directions. Arbitrarily, he pointed to one of the students and said, "You win." He waited a moment for the feeling of cheapness, unfairness, and slightedness to sink in before reaffirming this pedagogical nugget: without a clear outcome, whether students succeed or fail, they will always feel terrible. This is additionally true in games, where a victory via means that are misunderstood by the player is interpreted as a fluke, and the player learns nothing. This leads to interesting and confounding results in user research, which sometimes shows players succeeding on mission tasks, but reporting low satisfaction, having low arousal, and generally not having fun. This means providing clear goals to players from the start. While met with much vitriol on the Internet, the golden trail in *Fable II*™ kept players engaged by ensuring they had a clear objective. I would argue this could also be done through level design. Regardless, the goals and outcomes were clear from the beginning, which is of paramount importance in promoting flow experiences.

Summary

I hope that this chapter has given you some context on what makes players continue or stop playing your games. The various psychological factors should probably surprise you, as to most of us it seems automatic: either we like something or we don't. In the next chapter, I am going to talk about how we can differentiate groups of players along psychological lines, and how to make certain that our learning design is accommodating all of them to the greatest extent possible.

Cheat Sheet

Here is the cheat sheet of important items from this chapter; their definitions are given as they apply to games.

Arousal: One half of a method used to plot emotions in 2D space. Essentially, arousal illustrates how actively you are involved in something, or how much energy you are spending performing it.

Boredom: There is more to boredom than meets the eye. Psychologically, boredom occurs in a task when skill level greatly outweighs challenge, and valence and arousal are both low. In this case, players disengage because nothing is holding their attention. Occurs when high skill players are forced through tutorial levels, when no options to employ skills are present, or when players are simply not having fun.

Cognitive Apprenticeship: A theory of instruction that allows for "borrowing" of schema from an expert using modeling and scaffolding. It is modeled after traditional apprenticeship relationships. In games, this often takes the form of an expert AI that players are expected to emulate.

Flow: A state of "optimal experience" in which the player is learning and verifying that learning through performance objectives in near perfect harmony. An enjoyable experience, flow is characterized by loss of time perception, near perfect concentration, and exemplary performance on in-game objectives.

Frustration: An (often) undesirable emotional state resulting from an excess of arousal and low valence. Csikszentmihayli also believed that skill level played a part, in that a person with high arousal, low valence, and low skill level would be frustrated. Often occurs when players are not clearly conveyed goals and outcomes, controls are bungled, and so on. This is the result of a disconnect between the cognitively desired outcome and what is happening on screen.

Instructional Scaffolding: A method of instruction whereby support is offered at first, and then slowly removed as mastery is gained. An example might be helping students through problems until they get the gist, and then removing that support to verify that learning has occurred.

Just-In-Time Instruction: Refers to instruction or help given just before people are about to disengage due to cognitive overload. Trained teachers are able to observe this through subtle nuances in student cognition through years of observation and practice. For the rest of us, it is safe to assume that after more than a few screw-ups or undesirable outcomes, people are about to disengage.

Modeling: In education, modeling is the process of observing and replicating the behavior of an expert practitioner. "Okay, watch me do this. Now you try." Modeling is a necessary facet of cognitive apprenticeship.

Valence: The other half of a method used to plot emotions on a 2D graph. Valence describes things as desirable or undesirable, and is often mapped as the horizontal axis, although I suppose it doesn't matter.

5
FACTS ABOUT PLAYERS

It would take years of reading psychological manuscripts, theses, reports from governmental agencies, and literally sifting through mountains of data to come to a holistic understanding of what makes a player a player. While I can't claim to know everything about gamers, from years of work in human computer interaction and psychological research intersecting game design and software engineering, I have learned a lot. Again, some heavy psychology material here will be gathered up into a cheat sheet at the end of the chapter.

Unfortunately, in good research anyway, it is hard to delineate or list any clear facts about people as a whole. For this reason, this chapter is going to abandon that approach. Instead of trying to tell you the facts like "all gamers like tofu" or "gamers between the ages of 11 and 21 prefer cottage cheese rather than feta," I'm going to tell you one inalienable fact about gamers and people in general: factually, people differ significantly, but there are a few key things that we can use to bind them together and get a better understanding of our audience. More appropriately, this chapter will make you aware of the things that differentiate one player from another, and drive home exactly how important it is to account for these differences. If, for example, we performed our user testing without pre-tests, we would have no idea if we had accidentally recruited a group full of pro-gamers or a group full of people who had never touched a controller in their lives. While many companies do feature an "entry interview" for their play testing, I am going to demonstrate some of the more overlooked elements that contribute, psychologically, to our enjoyment or distaste for games.

A few things differentiate players of games. The obvious ones are researched to death—things like age, socioeconomic status, race, gender, and predisposition to games. There are entire schools of thought dedicated to researching stuff like this. It is important, necessary, and formative work that gives us data about our target populations. Unfortunately, these are way bigger topics than I can fit into this book. I also don't have the expertise to comment on a lot of them. However, education and cognitive psychology do give us many generalities about the human mind that transcend these sorts of characteristics. If you want to truly understand your audience, I'd recommend checking out the further reading in the Appendix at the back of the book and reading up on some other authors who are doing amazing work regarding demographic and personal characteristics and consumption of games. For now, I will talk about a few constants of the mind that will affect how players solve the problems in your game, learn from them, and play them.

A type of psychology sometimes called *individual differences psychology* focuses on the differences between human beings while still establishing some constant psychological effects. Again, this is beyond the scope of the book, but it is definitely worth some further study. Individual differences psychology tells us that parts of the human being that are independent of our treatment (in this case, the treatment is the video game) are going to affect how the person reacts to what we present. In traditional psychological research, we gather as much data as is humanly possible so that after the fact we can analyze it for correlations and linkages. This means that it is entirely conceivable, for example, that eye color could be correlated with desire for chocolate, right-handedness could be correlated with the urge to become a mad scientist, and so on. These things are largely out of our control. There are some things, however, that are not.

Psychologists are interested in how the individual sees and perceives the world. Often, preferences in problem solving, interpersonal communication, and social skills are interrogated using psychometric tests. One such test that illustrates the differences and similarities between players is called the *Myers-Briggs Type Indicator,** or MBTI. The MBTI is a type of test that divides peoples' personalities into different letters, which represent different elements of thinking and problem solving. There is a very good chance you have taken one of these during your life as part of a job or career placement test. Results

---

* Briggs Myers, I. (1988). *Gifts differing: Understanding personality type.* Mountain View, CA: Consulting Psychologists Press.

tend to fall in four-letter initialisms, like ENFP (for me) or INTJ (for some other person). These letters are compiled across four planes that offer us insight into a variety of elements of the human mind. If we are able to understand these planes, we can apply that knowledge to the design of challenges and obstacles in our games that will teach our players how to continue having fun, completing challenges, and playing our games. I would like to keep one thing constant throughout this discussion: chances are, you are reading this thinking of implementing some of these psychological tidbits into your user testing or research, which is awesome. I would like to point out that this is just one of many tests you can apply to your games testers before gathering data from them in order to ensure a truly random sample, one of the hallmarks of good research.

The first and most easily observable of the four parts of this model is the attitude scale, which determines whether people are given to introversion or extraversion. Introverts are typically quiet and reserved and prefer to act in solitary situations. Contrarily, those who are extraverted are attention seeking, loud, and incredibly outgoing. Different cultures place different values on introversion and extraversion. In North America, having a big voice and being outgoing are considered assets, whereas in Japan, introversion is considered to be respectful, polite, and dignified. Why does this matter to games? Very simple—consider the introvert for a moment. How likely is he or she to want to be the singer, or participate at all, in a game like *Rock Band*? The answer is probably *not very*, unless alone or in certain situations. It is a chore for people who are introverted to interact with large groups of people in social situations. On the other hand, how much fun is a true extrovert going to get from a visual novel? Bear in mind that these type indicators are not hard guarantees of whether someone is going to like something. The methods by which players choose their likes and dislikes are complicated and far-reaching. I am only here to show you the differences in how people solve problems, so that you might have some insight in your design choices and user testing.

The second of the MBTI parameters is the letter responsible for the intake of data. This is important to games, as often our primary mode of teaching players to solve problems in our designs is to give them data about the situation, the controls, and the context of the game world. These portions are divided into sense or intuition. These two data-gathering methods differentiate people in how they "read" a situation. Those individuals who tend to *sense* want very clear instruction on just about everything. If the player with a sensing disposition cannot see clear data in their instructions, he or she is not going to learn anything. On the other hand, those individuals who prefer *intuition* are more given to theory and abstract data. Hidden methods of teaching, such as the discovery learning method we have discussed, will be more effective with these people. In game design, it is therefore important to triangulate our methods of education and learning design to make sure that both individuals who gather data concretely as well as abstractly can be accommodated in their learning. This involves offering tips and pop-ups for the concrete learner, and discovery learning for the theoretical learner. How is this possible? Well, scaffolded instructions that look for learners to make mistakes before inundating them with pop-ups is one option, and there are many others. We will talk about a lot of them in Chapter 8.

The third MBTI category is concerned with how individuals solve problems. Again, this is important to our game development process as the fundamental difference between games and films is that the user must solve problems or overcome obstacles in order to advance the narrative, in many cases. If we look at games like *BEYOND: Two Souls* that feature narrative and cinematic heavy cut scenes and storytelling, it can sometimes blur the line between the two, which is indicative of the evolution of the medium, in my opinion. In any case, this third portion of the MBTI is divided into *thinking* and *feeling*. These two things differentiate how people apply the information that they have gathered in the previous indicator to the solving of complex issues in their lives, jobs, and so on. Thinking individuals make logical decisions based on a third-person assessment of a situation. They are the "lawful neutrals" of the psychology world—they will often make a rational assessment based on quantitative and neutral data. On the other hand, the feeling individuals tend to make their decisions based on personal association. They put themselves in the place of the problem, and feel through the situation accordingly. Ever wonder why a game that is technically, artistically, and mechanically solid still has dissenters? Welcome to the world of individual differences psychology. No matter how solid your design is, someone, somewhere, will not like it; and this particular branch of psychology does its best to quantify and identify individuals, so you don't waste resources designing for folks who aren't going to like what you're selling anyway. They will be different for every game project, but rest assured, there is a game out there you will simply not like based on your personal predilections, no matter how mechanically perfect it might be.

Finally, the last letter of the MBTI deals with how individuals guide their lifestyle. This section is divided into *judging* or *perceiving*. This determines how people deal with individuals in the outside world. More important to multiplayer games, this key difference in individuals determines whether people are more likely to expose their problem-solving skill or their data-gathering skill. It is somewhat complicated, but individuals who are judgers will show their problem-solving skills to others in an attempt to resolve interpersonal conflicts, whereas those who are perceivers will show the world their information-gathering skills in order to solve such problems. If you had to negotiate a raise with your boss, which would you show? Would you illustrate all the industry data you have gathered on what your job ought to be worth, or would you show all of the concrete things you have added to the company? Why does this matter to game design? This is a tough one and only relates to multiplayer, but the takeaway is that individuals need to be considered when designing multiplayer games. *World of Warcraft* and other MMOs do a great job of this by allowing users to segment themselves into user roles. Everyone adds to the team in the way that he or she is personally most comfortable. This is one of the many secrets to the success of online multiplayer RPGs.

Every individual player has a whole host of differences. Psychometric tests like the MBTI allow us to quantify those differences. If you work for a company, does your company's user research and business analytics team pre-test its volunteers for what kind of MBTI they might be? If not, how can they be sure they are not filling a room with only ENTPs and getting useless data? This is but one of many things we can do to triangulate our data methods and change our teaching accordingly. I think this chapter is going to show you that a lot of difference really does exist between different game players and, as a result, we are fortunate to have entertained as many people as we have without considering it.

Age and the Education Gap

This is probably one of the most important parts of this book. The average game player has aged significantly in the last few years, and is now well over 30 years old. Because of this, it is a logical next step that individuals who are gaming now grew up with games. I went over this a bit in the introduction. As games increase in complexity, and more particularly as game consoles increase in complexity from the one-button interface of the *Atari 2600* to the modern console, education needs to ramp up accordingly. However, many of those individuals who are making games grew up alongside them, and are familiar and learned in the natural progression to which they were personally privy. Unfortunately, that is something that can't be replicated. An individual now attempting to play a game who has no prior experience must start with complicated equipment in the vast majority of cases. New gamers who are being born and growing up to play games are starting with a higher learning curve than we ever did.

On the other end of the age discussion, getting older people involved in technology is a huge concern with a large body of research surrounding it; however, little research has been done on attempting to approach geriatrics to get them to play *Call of Duty* and scream obscenities into microphones. That said, it is clear that there is an age differential in what constitutes game playership. This age differential extends in both directions, as new gamers are often getting their start on touch-capacitive devices as opposed to traditional controllers like those that you might see on the *Xbox*™. Maybe this is a pathway to simpler controls that will allow the next generation to get used to lower element interactivity before advancing to traditional games? In any case, there is no excuse not to refine our teaching.

Both Piaget and Vygotsky teach us that there are discrete, different stages to the development of the mind.[*] This is relevant to game design: depending on the audience for whom we are designing our games, our tutorial interventions have to change accordingly. In the Piagetian tradition, people move from a very basic level of mental operations in childhood to a more concrete and realistic method of thinking in adulthood. The level of cognition varies from person to

---

[*] Piaget, J. (1951). *The psychology of intelligence*. London: Routledge Publishers.

person, and Piaget himself didn't truly understand exactly when each stage started and ended down to the day. Consequently, these elements of human development serve as a blueprint for how humans learn rather than hard instructions.

While the dates that Piaget specified have been studied rigorously and often found to be more of a general indicator than an exact number, this should demonstrate a larger point: age is an important factor in testing users who play our games. If we don't account for that individual difference, even down to a few years, there is a multitude of reasons we could be getting ugly data. Not only do users of different age groups have different experiences in growing up with (or without) video games, but there is also an element of psychological development that changes as our players age that may make certain things palatable and others distasteful.

(Experience + Skill)/Challenge = Fun

I won't spend an enormous amount of time on this point, as it is almost always included, in some incarnation, in the text of people's entry interviews. Prior experience in game playership plays an enormous role in future enjoyment of games. When completing my Ph.D., I made certain to seek out people who had never before played a game so that I could be sure that their schemata for games were nonexistent. For example, if we attempt to create three or four different tutorial methods with the intention of testing them between players, experience is a necessary interrogation in any entry interview. Imagine, for example, that one tutorial treatment, through random selection, was assigned a group of people who had extensive history playing games. It would appear in data as though this group was amazingly more successful than the others were, and the logical assertion from that would be that this tutorial was better than all the others were in some way. Unfortunately, tainted data like this are worse than nothing. A good principle to remember is poor data are worse than no data.

Again, since this is an area of game testing that is rather well developed—companies tend to interrogate the previous play experiences of their testers before recruiting them—I won't spend too much space beating a dead horse. One thing I would like to elucidate, though, is the importance of recognizing whether experiences with games were positive and successful or negative and unsuccessful, and there are some very good reasons for this.

It Is Never Okay to Throw the Controller

One important factor to consider when discussing prior experiences with games is prior negative experiences with games, and how these can code our interaction with future games in the same genre. We talked a little bit about the things that cause players to stop playing games in Chapter 4. Particularly, I tried to highlight the importance of both frustration and boredom in preventing people from continuing to play your game. These are important factors, as measuring them can give you meaningful insight into when players are about to quit playing. The level to which players will tolerate punishment is directly proportional to their previous experiences with gaming, which you can't control. Let me elucidate this point a bit. An individual who has been through a terrible business failure is going to be more likely to identify patterns that will lead to business failure in the future. So too will an individual who has had negative experiences with gaming in the past, such as being unable to learn or perform game outcomes despite his or her best efforts, identify patterns in games as leading to negative outcomes. Eventually, the player's tolerance for game punishment will approach zero, and he or she will literally balk from playing games that punish him or her at the first sight of such treatment. On the other hand, an individual who has had repeated successes in gaming is more likely to blame the game for problems. "I'm not bad, this game is bad. Why should I be treated like this? I'll show this game: I'll keep playing it until I beat it." That is not to say that experienced gamers are invincible. Even the most erudite of gamers will eventually throw the controller down in disgust if they are abused repeatedly.

Unlike the other elements of individual differences psychology I have mentioned in this chapter, this factor can be investigated in-game without being invasive and asking questions about age, sex, and so on. Low tolerance to failure is something we can definitely detect. Suppose a simple data point is dropped every time a person dies, every time a person saves, and every time a person turns off the game (perhaps by placing a data point every time a game is loaded successfully—you would only see this data point after a game had been reset, turned off, or the power had gone out). We can correlate data very nicely here. If a person dies once or twice and then a load event is recorded, it is obvious that the player is turning the game off in frustration after having failed only once or twice. On the other hand, if a play session including many deaths has a negative correlation with loads, this would indicate that our player base finds challenge motivating, and that we should go ahead and open the floodgates on the wholesale murder of our fans. Go for it—rip their heads off.

Correlating data points like this can help us identify the educational gap between different groups of players. It is very easy to discount data as outlier effects—100 or 200 people among millions stop playing after a certain event, for example. More likely, this is a factor of the individual differences in our players. Pre-existing psychological data, measured in devious ways, can help us achieve this goal. How do we get this? With clever hooks. Give the player a quest and record everything he or she does. How does the player solve problems? Does the player walk up to NPCs and engage them in conversation? That allows us to profile the player as an extrovert to some degree. On top of that, we can make meaningful observations about the player by using the game world. What is the speed at which the player completes quests? Does the player accept every quest given to him or her? Why do you think that happens? Is the player driven by conscientiousness, greed, or achievement?

The Big Five Motivational Factors and Games

In a talk at GDC 2012, Jason VanderBerghe drew some correlations between what are known as the Big Five Motivational Factors and game development.[*] I think that is brilliant. I am going to take it a step further and say that you should be interrogating these motivational factors as part of the standard interview process by which you recruit your game testers, along with an MBTI, as well as a full workup on their prior experiences with games, good or bad. The Big Five Factors are

---

[*] VanderBerghe, J. (2012). Applying psychology principles to game design. Game Developer's Conference 2012.

derived from a theory called the five-factor model,[*] which maps personality traits. I am not going to suggest that these traits map directly to game design objectives, as this isn't really a book on game design. Rather, I am just going to suggest that you know what these five factors are, know that it is important to control for them in your testing, and know that there are established metrics for measuring them. The five factors are generally considered to be openness to experience, conscientiousness, extraversion, agreeableness, and neuroticism.

Openness to experience is exactly as it sounds. Individuals who possess this trait are given to experiential hedonism. New things are their motivation. When they can explore, discover, or otherwise pave new roads, they are at their happiest. Next on the list is conscientiousness, which indicates those individuals who are driven by a motivation to succeed. A conscientious game player might be eager to show off his or her achievements, whether literal or figurative, in a game. This player will also benefit from games that allow him or her to excel. Next is extraversion, which is also exactly as it sounds. Extroverted individuals prefer situations through which they can garner social contacts and connections, as we have discussed. These individuals are more likely to draw motivation from social sources. Agreeableness maps a need for cooperation and team building. Highly agreeable individuals will prefer activities in which everyone can get along and there is little sense of competition or conquest. Finally, neuroticism maps how likely individuals are to perceive negative consequences. A highly neurotic individual will make a "mountain out of a molehill" and react very negatively to seemingly benign punishments. While these do have implications for game design, I would rather point you to the tests in the footnote, the NEO-FFI instrument used to measure these big five factors. This should be standard in the recruitment of your testers.

Summary

With any luck, this chapter has demonstrated to you that it is hard to make any major generalizations about players. However, there are

---

[*] Costa, P. & McCrae, R. (1992). *Revised NEO personality inventory (NEO-PI-R) and NEO five-factor inventory (NEO-FFI) manual.* Odessa, FL: Psychological Assessment Resources.

several instances in which differences are the same among people. I have given you a few methods of analyzing these differences through individual differences psychology, such as the MBTI and Five-Factor Model. You also read about how age and previous experiences can code future experiences with games. The next chapter will discuss how the brain handles audio and video in importantly different ways, and how you can capitalize on that in your learning design.

Cheat Sheet

Here is the chapter's cheat sheet. Like always, please feel free to use this as a reference sheet. The terms used in the chapter are defined here as they relate to game design.

Big Five Personality Traits: Part of a five-factor model of human motivation. Openness to experience, conscientiousness, extraversion, agreeableness, and neuroticism (OCEAN). Differentiates people by their source of motivation and is another excellent metric for differentiating our player base.

Focus Groups: An antiquated method of user testing where individuals would sit around a room and discuss questions about the product or game as directed by an expert. Subject to all sorts of psychological biases. Can result in biased data.

Individual Differences Psychology: This is a branch of psychology devoted to deriving the differences between individuals that run constant across all of humanity. Relevance to game design involves making certain that all manner of people can be pleased by our games. It also has major implications for recruiting our testers to ensure you have a truly random sample.

Myers-Briggs Type Indicator: An instrument used to differentiate people across their attitude, information gathering, problem solving, and lifestyle preferences. Contains a four-letter indicator like ENFP or INTJ. An excellent method to differentiate the preferences of our audiences in a cost-effective and rapid manner.

6
EYES AND EARS

After decades of multimedia, games, film, and art studies crossing disciplines, one thing has become certain; people parse visual information and auditory information differently. Video games are blessed with access to both of these channels, plus physical input through a controller. It just so happens that the brain has separate handlers for each of these things, and by learning how to take advantage of that, we can promote flow and positive engagement in our games. This chapter boils down research on multiple channel theories of how the brain parses information into readable actionable tidbits, and then demonstrates how visual and auditory elements are presented and used in contemporary games. It finishes by linking this back to the tutorial system, and how it can help players prepare for the images and sounds to be used in the game in question. As usual, some talk about the various parts of the brain and how they handle information is going to be undertaken, and it is going to be a little heavy, so I will finish the chapter with a cheat sheet review.

Visual Stuff in Games

As is the case with most media, we are obsessed with how things look. Our eyes dominate our sensory perception in most video games, and this preoccupation with all things visual often leads to us making a mess of the screen in an attempt to cram in a lot of information.

This makes me think back to my *World of Warcraft* experiences. Often times I would need so much information to perform my role as a tank skillfully, that I would literally have to splatter the screen with dials, indicators, icons, counters, and more. Any novice looking at this screen would be completely overwhelmed by the sheer amount of information that was presented to them. On top of that, I noticed that I, as a skilled player, was starting to ignore some aspects of the visual display as well. I came across an amazing mod called NAO, which told me when to use certain abilities as a Warrior; it did this, however, with sound. No on-screen display, just a loud noise when it was time to hit a certain button.

In addition to the game field, other elements of a game are portrayed visually. The interface, the in-game instructions, and the controller itself are all visual artifacts. When you try to remember which is the *X* and which is the *Y* button on a *Super Nintendo* controller, it is likely that you are visually recalling it, although I admit that some of you will use haptic or motor memory—how it feels.

The vast majority of information in digital games is presented to the players through their eyes, which does a disservice to the medium. This preoccupation with the visual sense is by no means limited to games. The movie industry, advertising, art, and much of the world in which we live consist of visual display. Take a few moments in the neon-soaked streets of Tokyo or in awe at the cinematography of a summer blockbuster as commonsense examples. As we learned in Chapter 3 and as we are going to learn here, there is a special way that the brain handles each individual sense. In the case of digital games, we have audio and visual to work with, with some haptic stuff in the use of the vibration motors in the controller. For the sake of the educational psychology sort of hook that this book is taking, I will focus only on the areas where there is a lot of research, namely, video and audio.

Audible Stuff in Games

The other half of a game's presentation is, of course, what you can hear. For the vast majority of game projects, this means the background music and various sound effects. There is really not much else to say here. Game design dating back to the arcade eras didn't always have music, other than a jingle to signify that the level had begun; think *Pac-Man*, for example. It was uncommon for there to be a music track on early home systems as well, partially because of memory limitations, and partially because the best sounds coming out of very early games could barely produce anything resembling music.

We have learned an amazing amount about how to make music and sounds. As a result, in modern games, there are several approaches to audio. Occasionally, sounds are used to cue attention; we will talk about this more in the following section. Auditory cueing takes the form of 3D sound telling us from which direction we are taking fire, or loud noises pointing our attention a certain way. In *World of Warcraft*, for example, a quick jingling noise lets you know when a pop-up, tutorial or otherwise, has appeared on the screen. This is an effective way to offload some of the visual load associated with *World of Warcraft*'s already heavy visual interface. Other times, sound is used in a cinematic way. Background music (BGM) frames the action, while sound effects punctuate our experience. This is the case in games such as *Heavy Rain* or the *UNCHARTED* series. In still other cases, music is used in a retro game design sense; BGM pours out of the game seemingly irrespective of onscreen action. This is reminiscent of games like *Super Mario Bros.* or *The Legend of Zelda* where the music would pipe out regardless of what was happening on screen, depending only on the level or area. Games like this are *Terraria*™ or *Rogue Legacy*. Some games have no BGM to speak of, like *Kerbal Space Program*, although at the time of writing, it is still in beta so, who knows!

Finally, one meaningful use of sound in game design is to punctuate action or change the mood of the title. Games like *Flower*, *Journey*, and *Minecraft* make excellent use of various types of music to induce moods in the player. Games like *Hotline Miami*™ punctuate their frenetic murder sprees with sudden silence, letting you take a moment to retroactively analyze what you have done, as you silently step out over throngs of splattered bodies in unsettling quiet. Unfortunately, sound is rarely used to enhance education in games—to teach the players how to play—with some exceptions that I have mentioned earlier in the book.

Why Does This Matter?

We have already talked a bit about the Attentional Control Theory, the Dual Coding Theory, and the Cognitive Theory of Multimedia Learning in Chapter 3. In this chapter, I would like to highlight a key element in all three: audio and video are handled differently by our minds. Learning theories differ, but the one I believe that best applies to game design is Richard Mayer's cognitive theory, particularly its various principles.

This is by no means new information. Education scholars, psychologists, and cognitive scientists have known for a while now that the mind processes audio and video on different channels. My first introduction to this concept came from Paivio's dual coding theory, which has been mentioned throughout. Dual coding theory states that all data are stored as either a word or a picture. Ergo, we store our mental "data," if you will, in the form of images and sounds, or at least verbal representations of sounds. Under this theory, if I'm able to get you to remember both the image and the sound of the instructions on how to play a game, you will be more likely to remember it later than if I only gave you one of those two things. This isn't always strictly sound and pictures; for example, the word *gun* and a picture of a gun are fine as an image and a "sound," even if they are both on paper. To clarify this mix-up, Paivio called the two things *imagens* and *logogens* to differentiate them as pictures and words, and not strictly sounds and sights.

Other theories deal with working memory. Working memory is the part of your brain that is actively working on sensory input to make sense of it, relate it to existing schema or make new ones as necessary, and then add it to your long-term memory stores. We know that this is limited by a few things that we've discussed, like cognitive load and the magic number.

As the various theories wrought in years of academic work have shown us, and as I discussed in Chapter 3, there is much debate about how the mind processes and stores information. Despite these academic disagreements, however, there are a few things about memory and information processing that we know really well.

First, sound and audio have their own dedicated processing centers (see Figure 6.1). These are referred to in Baddeley and later as the visuospatial sketchpad for visual traces and the phonological loop for auditory traces. These act like a sound studio and an art studio. Phonological things like words and sounds are recorded and processed as sound and associated to and from schema appropriately. Visual things, much the same, are processed and associated where they are needed in the schemata of the long-term memory. Because these two parts of the mind are distinct, all information brought in from video and sound are processed separately; if the two are presented simultaneously, they must be separated first and processed second, which incurs load.

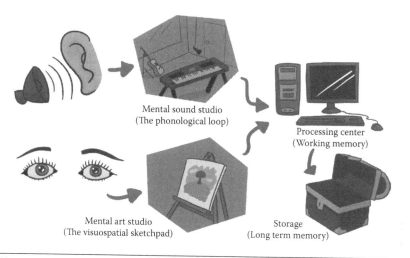

Figure 6.1 Human memory diagram. (Figure courtesy of Peter Kalmar.)

Second, the load that it takes to run the phonological loop and the visuospatial sketchpad is additive. That is to say, every sound and symbol that has to be processed in working memory takes up some of your very limited cognitive resources. For this reason, it is important to think carefully about our uses for sound. Mann's attentional control theory also comes with an instructional design model called the Structured Sound Functions (SSF) model, which provides key uses for sound in multimedia education. The boiled-down version is that every little bit of sound we add on to something takes up a little more of our cognitive resources. After a while, a natural filtering effect takes place, in which certain information is prioritized or ignored. Which information is prioritized and which is ignored, unfortunately, can be unpredictable. Imagine for a moment the effect of being in a crowded subway. You will have visual and spatial indicators, such as other people moving around, signs lighting and dimming, trains moving, advertisements, and so on. On top of that, there are auditory indicators: the screech of trains, the PA system, other people talking, footsteps, and more. You know logically that you are hearing and seeing all of these things, but much of it is filtered. For example, if after exposing you to this hypothetical crowded agoraphobic nightmare I were to ask you, "At which minute, out of the ten you were in the subway, did you hear the clicking of high-heeled shoes?", I would be willing to bet that you would be unable to answer. In fact, I would bet you would be unsure whether you heard them at all. This is a natural effect that our brain uses to prevent cognitive overload. Trying to focus on all of those things at once would be maddening; your brain literally can't handle it all. As a result, things are filtered out. In our games, as complexity increases without appropriate learning, mechanics of the game are filtered out as well. This could include the movement, how to avoid enemies, which fingers to place on which buttons, and more—it's unpredictable!

Third, and somewhat related to the previous point, information is grouped based on proximal relevance. Consistent with dual coding theory, when things are either cognitively "close together" or cognitively "very far apart," they are easier to remember. One is useful to games, the other not so much. Let's start with the useful one—proximity. Mayer discusses this in the principles I'll outline next, but suffice to say individuals remember things that are proximal to one another as a group, or chunk, instead of discrete elements. In an example from Gestalt Theory,

a. 1, 4, 3

b. 143

You likely verbalize item *a* as "one, four, three" and item *b* as "one hundred forty-three." So what? Well, Gestalt Theory states that proximal items are encoded as a group, and based on what we know about cognitive load and limits on the human memory, that should tell us something important: it takes less load to remember item *b* than item *a*. In game design, there are a few obvious places for this—one might be placing the ammo display right next to the gun display. We will talk more about that next; suffice to say, things that are (cognitively) closer together are remembered as a group.

The less useful effect in this series is called the von Restorff effect.[*] When an object is cognitively "out of place" among other objects, it will be easier to recall. While this could be used to some interesting artistic ends, I'm not sure how it would apply directly to game design. Essentially, the von Restorff effect illustrates the following: if I were to give you a list of items that all had a common theme, like "classroom,"

---

[*] The classical literature is in German, so check out Fabiani, M. & Donchin, E. (1995). Encoding processes and memory organization: A model of the von Restorff effect. *Journal of Experimental Psychology: Learning, Memory, and Cognition,* 21(1).

then the word "spoon" would be more readily recalled in the first list than in the second. This is because it is in isolation as compared to the second list. In a similar fashion, if you were to walk into a classroom and observe a chainsaw sitting on a desk, it is unlikely you would forget it.

LIST 1	LIST 2
Chalkboard	Knife
Desk	Plate
Board Marker	Fork
Spoon	Spoon
Lectern	Pot

While dual coding theory as well as the psychological effects discussed here talk about long-term memory being stored in words and pictures and recalled more easily if it is held in both, other theories are more relevant to game design. These deal with the working memory as well as long-term memory, although not to discount Paivio's work because it was definitely foundational and transformational! Mayer's cognitive theory has a series of principles that best demonstrate how we can use elements of multimedia to solidify learning. It is my strong opinion from being an educator and game designer that these can be meaningfully applied to game design with an understanding of how the eyes and ears process information differently, and the psychological effects that this causes.

Mayer's Principles: Designing Learning for Our Eyes and Ears

Core to Mayer's Cognitive Theory of Multimedia Learning is the inclusion of several principles. These principles demonstrate different things about how we can best make multimedia displays line up with the cognitive architecture of the human mind. Of course, it sounds like these might be design principles, and, in my opinion, that's awesome. The principles and concepts contained in the cognitive theory are extrapolated from years of research and understanding of what constitutes good multimedia learning. This, of course, is bolstered by both psychological and neurological studies of how the brain handles the eyes and the ears. Mayer's principles can be directly mapped to game design concepts, and that is what I would like to talk about here, as I think it is most relevant to you, the reader. If you want to read further, the Appendix has a lot of good information on where you can find heavy psychological stuff to pore over. There are more than eight widely accepted principles, but I think these eight best relate to game design. Feel free to check out the further reading to research the other ones, too.

Multimedia Principle

First of Mayer's principles, the multimedia principle demonstrates that a combination of words through either writing or audio, along with images and graphics, is intrinsically better at teaching than either of those things is alone. This means that a picture with accompanying text, like the popular Internet infographic, is going to be easier to remember than just the picture itself, or just the text itself. From a commonsense standpoint, this is understandable. When, in infancy, we first begin to learn things, we are presented with both the subject, such as opening a bottle, and expert instruction in the form of words and images from our parent or caretaker. In games, this means that a combination effect is necessary to effectively teach players to play the game. Both the mechanics and the tips should line up to teach a consistent message. Here is an example for a generic FPS game; pay close attention to the tense shift in the language:

VIOLATES THE MULTIMEDIA PRINCIPLE	ADOPTS THE MULTIMEDIA PRINCIPLE
"Enemies *will* shoot at you! If you're hit, make sure to take cover while your health regenerates."	"You are *being* shot! Notice your health *is depleting*! Take cover to let it regenerate!"
Action: Paused	Action: Ongoing
Pop-up: Visual	Pop-up: Auditory

By allowing the action to take place as the tutorials are happening, we accept the multimedia principle that text indicating something (*damage*) is happening while an image (*actually seeing the damage happen, red jelly on the screen*) accompanies it.

Modality Principle

The modality principle is probably the easiest of all to implement into game projects. Modality tells us that learners are better at remembering and understanding instructions when they are presented as speech rather than as text or writing. Games are notorious for disobeying this rule in their tutorial systems. Known to educators and educative multimedia designers, game designers can grab this principle by making a simple switch. As an interesting note, I replicated this principle in my Ph.D. thesis and, indeed, it did help gamers stay engaged longer and make fewer errors. Consider the following example from a generic MMORPG:

VIOLATES THE MODALITY PRINCIPLE	ADOPTS THE MODALITY PRINCIPLE
"This is a potion. Drink it to restore health by right-clicking on the icon."	"This is a potion. Drink it to restore health by right-clicking on the icon."
Action: Ongoing	Action: Ongoing
Pop-up: Visual	Pop-up: Auditory

Coherence Principle

This one is a little tough for game designers. Ultimately, the coherence principle states "don't bombard the learner," or players will learn better when extraneous stuff is excluded rather than included. A bunch of beeping sounds makes an audio cue to attention easy to miss, for example. A jumbled interface could make a pop-up get lost in visual memory. Because of game design trends, it is very common to see a lot of information on screen at any given time, although games with a very thin interface, such as *Flower*, are also popular. Audio is no less jumbled, as music, sounds, beeps, and whirs are shot at our ears on a near second-by-second level. I would argue that the coherence principle best applies to game design in terms of the challenges necessary to continue. If we use level design and mechanic implementation to make sure that players are only encountering things relevant to the current learning objective, we will succeed in teaching them. Consider the following example from a generic platformer:

VIOLATES THE COHERENCE PRINCIPLE	ADOPTS THE COHERENCE PRINCIPLE
Level 1-1 is a cloud level with platforms that will teach the player the jumping and flying mechanics of *Super Lemur Man*.	Level 1-1 is a ground-based level with pitfalls designed to teach the player the jumping mechanics, while Level 1-2 depicts *Lemur Man's* ascent into the skies to instruct the player in flying.
Action: Ongoing	Action: Ongoing
Pop-up: N/A	Pop-up: N/A

Segmenting Principle

This is an easy principle: break complex things down into smaller steps. If we consider *Super Mario World*™ for the *Super Nintendo Entertainment System*™, we know that the cape allows us to do many things. It allows us to fly, but also controls our ascent and descent, and lets us kill things with our big Italian plumber belly. This is really a multipart process, however. Running has to happen first, which constitutes pressing a direction and holding down the run button. When a certain speed is reached, the player has to jump into the air; at this point, control shifts from traditional platforming controls to an effective up-and-down control to ascend or descend. Ultimately, the entire principle boils down to "break things into smaller steps where possible." Consider this breakdown for how to fly in *Super Mario World*:

VIOLATES THE SEGMENTING PRINCIPLE	ADOPTS THE SEGMENTING PRINCIPLE
Infographic showing the feather item, the cape appearing on *Mario*'s back, and him flying into the sky.	Infographic showing the feather item and cape appearing on *Mario*. Followed by this is a controller overlay showing what to press to make *Mario* run. The next fading image shows *Mario* in midair with the new controls illustrated.

Pre-training Principle

This is a good one, but it seems like we stumble over it an awful lot. The pre-training principle tells us that people need to have complex material with high element interactivity broken down into key terms or concepts, that might otherwise be referred to as jargon. Essentially, until a learner has significant schemata surrounding a particular topic, he or she has to pull out each concept piece by piece, which can very quickly cause a cognitive overload, which isn't fun (sort of the antithesis of what you want out of game design, unless you're a sadist). Pre-training means that people need information before complex topics come and broadside them, and we are generally pretty good at providing this in games in the form of tutorial levels and pop-ups; however, we often violate enough of the other principles that the learning doesn't stick. Look at the following example from a generic JRPG:

VIOLATES THE PRE-TRAINING PRINCIPLE	ADOPTS THE PRE-TRAINING PRINCIPLE
You gained a level! Open the menu to level up your character and select new skills and attributes.	1. Your character became stronger and gained an experience level! Open the menu with A. 2. New levels mean new skills and attributes, press B to assign points. 3. These are your skills and attributes.

Personalization Principle

The personalization principle dictates that learners understand material that is presented in a conversational tone better than material that is dictated to them in a traditional or didactic fashion. In game design, this means we have to make sure that our instructions try not to break the fourth wall too much—unless it is intentional, of course—and that we are not dictating to the player, either in our text or auditory instructions. This can be applied by using a conversational tone, or in-character voice-overs to direct players to particular actions or behaviors. Overly stilted language creates additional cognitive load and makes learning more difficult than it needs to be. Consider the following example from a generic MOBA type game:

VIOLATES THE PERSONALIZATION PRINCIPLE	ADOPTS THE PERSONALIZATION PRINCIPLE
In order to use a character's skills, the player must input a Q, W, E, or R keystroke. In turn, the player must also activate movement with the mouse, which will elicit forward, aft, starboard, or retrograde movement of the player-avatar in game space.	Greetings champion! Take the keys and send your minions to battle with the mouse. Fire your deadly spells with the Q W E R keys. Triumph and untold doom await!

Redundancy Principle

Because we know that the brain processes audio and video along different channels, and we know that the load incurred by doing this is additive, it is important that we not cognitively overload our players by wasting cognitive space on things that are redundant. Specifically, Mayer's redundancy principle states that human beings incur additional cognitive load when they are presented pictures on screen with accompanying simultaneous audio and text. Meaning, if you are going to design a video game and provide on-screen instructions to players, either narrate them or write them, but not both. Consider the following example from a generic sandbox action game:

VIOLATES THE REDUNDANCY PRINCIPLE	ADOPTS THE REDUNDANCY PRINCIPLE
Press the R2 or L2 button to switch weapons. Be careful, *Bill* will not automatically reload when switching weapons!	Press the R2 or L2 button to switch weapons. Be careful, *Bill* will not automatically reload when switching weapons!
Action: Ongoing	Action: Ongoing
Pop-up: Text with narration	Pop-up: None, just narration.

Contiguity Principle

The last of the principles, the contiguity principle, tells us that learners best absorb information when things are proximal to one another. For example, if I were to label my programming code with *//see comment 6*, then endnote comment, this is less efficient than just putting the comment inline. In game design, this means keeping relevant information close to the information upon which it depends. If that is confusing, this means keeping text or audio about what things do either proximally or temporally close to the object in question. This should make sense; it is harder to remember something when you have to look it up, than when the information is right there. Consider the following example from a generic first-person shooter:

VIOLATES THE CONTIGUITY PRINCIPLE	ADOPTS THE CONTIGUITY PRINCIPLE
Weapon info on left side of screen (type of gun). Ammo on right side of screen (bullets in clip).	Both pieces of info proximal on the right side of the screen.

Summary

After reading all of this, I hope you have some idea of how it works. It is important to understand the differences between how the brain handles sound and how it handles imagery. Because cognitive load is additive, it is important to always keep load from each sense as low as possible. Unfortunately, there have been no studies (of which I am aware) that have asked whether adding vibration or physical stuff increases load. In either case, we can make best use of our psychological understanding of how audio and video are processed by making sure to obey Mayer's principles as they apply to game design. Following this is a cheat sheet of everything we have covered in this chapter.

Cheat Sheet

Here is the cheat sheet of important items from the chapter; their definitions are given as they apply to games.

Attention Cueing: Using sound or images to grab attention. In class, the teacher uses his or her voice, the lights, pictures or images, and so on. In a multimedia presentation—like a game—sound cueing is often used. A loud noise cues attention to a particular object, like the jingling noise for tutorials in *World of Warcraft*.

Cognitive Load: A method of understanding how much mental processing one can handle at any given moment. Think of it as load on a computer processor. The fact is the human brain has limited processing capacity and can't (yet) be upgraded. All cognitive load from all sources is additive and contributes to cognitive overload.

Cognitive Overload: The process by which the brain is trying to handle too many things at once. When cognitive overload occurs, the brain first attempts to prevent it by filtering out things it considers irrelevant. If this is unsuccessful, the result is disengagement.

Cognitive Theory of Multimedia Learning: Richard Mayer's theory regarding how humans learn from multimedia. It is based on a solid understanding of the different cognitive processing capabilities of the eyes and ears; as such, it is the basis for this chapter.

Coherence Principle: Everything that is presented to the player needs to be relevant so you don't bombard them. When learning is intense, cut the music and on-screen junk back. Break learning into pieces so that learners aren't overloaded by extraneous data.

Contiguity Principle: The contiguity principle tells us that relevant information should be as close to the point of application as possible. In games, keep the ammo display near the guns, the item display near the point of pickup, and so on.

Gestalt Theory: Without going into the psychology, Gestalt Theory states that the brain has a tendency to organize things into "wholes." If I show you a negative space with a few images that kind of looks like a polar bear, you will form it into a polar bear, and recall the schema for polar bear.

Imagen: A component of Paivio's dual-coding theory. The imagen is a pseudo-visual representation of something you have seen or heard. It is a visual way to store data. Think about the visual portion of your memory of a cat—that's an imagen.

Logogen: The corollary component of Paivio's theory. The logogen is the verbal portion of the memory. If you again think of cat, it is both the written word c-a-t, and the sound "cat."

Magic Number: A limitation on human memory processing that stems from classical psychology. Miller discovered that people could only store seven (plus or minus two) things in their mind at a given moment; experiments continue to validate this theory.

Modality Principle: This one is easy: players will learn things more readily when they are presented as audio speech rather than on-screen text.

Multimedia Principle: The multimedia principle simply states that individuals will generally learn better from narrated audio accompanying images than text accompanying images.

Personalization Principle: In multimedia learning, this involves the use of avatars, on-screen advisors, and conversational speech. In games, this is extended to in-character speech. Conversational and in-character styles of text and conversation will teach players better than extraneous or stilted text.

Phonological Loop: The portion of working memory dedicated to sound. When you attempt to recall what a song sounds like, the sound a cow makes, or any other auditory trace, it is processed in the phonological loop. Like the visuospatial sketchpad, auditory traces here are added to total cognitive load.

Pre-training Principle: Individuals need to be trained ahead of time on complex topics so that they are aware of the jargon, terms, and cognitive chunks that they need to use to solve a problem. In games, this means incremental level design that allows the player to "chunk" skill sets appropriately.

Proximal Relevance: A cognitive effect that allows learners to more easily absorb things that are either temporally or physically proximal to one another. Seeing the map of the subway next to the subway train, for example, is easier to process and remember than putting it in the restroom.

Redundancy Principle: This principle dictates that good teaching requires multimedia presentations like games to choose either onscreen text or narrated audio, but not both at the same time. Because video and audio are processed differently, this will just increase cognitive load unnecessarily.

Schemata: The plural of the word *schema*.

Segmenting Principle: The segmenting principle indicates that all tutorial information should be broken down to as small a degree as is reasonably possible. Don't just show the NPC shooting the gun; instead, show him selecting his weapon, raising it, loading it, aiming, and firing.

Structured Sound Functions Model: An instructional design theory that provides clear uses for sound. The details of it are beyond the scope of this book, but it is referenced a lot in reading about audio. More about this can be found in the Appendix.

Visuospatial Sketchpad: The portion of working memory dedicated to processing visual information. If I ask you to picture a pumpkin, the part of your mind being used is the visuospatial sketchpad. Visual traces here are added to total cognitive load.

Von Restorff Effect: The effect of increasing memory when something "stands out." For example, if I were to place a bucket of applesauce in the middle of a hospital, you are more likely to remember it than, say, a medical cart.

Working Memory: A theory of Beddeley's. It is the portion of your brain that is essentially a "processor." Everything upon which you are currently concentrating occurs in the working memory. Both auditory and visual traces enter the working memory and contribute to overall cognitive load.

7

RETURN OF THE TUTORIAL: ESCAPE FROM SKULL ISLAND

In this chapter, we cook up an amusingly titled game with a familiar genre: action RPG. We create some mockups with pseudocode and art to allow the reader to see the different kinds of tutorials in action. All of the principles and discussion in the book are linked back to the game being built in this chapter, and put into the tutorials presented to the player. This understanding of tutorial elements is then reinforced by drawing links to current games employing great tutorials. By the end of the chapter, readers will be able to point out what constitutes well and poorly designed tutorials, and have a good idea about how to take these tutorials and put them into their game, without doing years of research on the topic.

This is a rather unique chapter in the book. As designers, you are probably familiar with game design documents, asset lists, and game flow diagrams. I am going to present to you here a type of (very light) game design document and synopsis for a hypothetical game called *Escape from Skull Island*. The purpose of this chapter isn't to make a good action RPG, although, hey, maybe I could publish this and make billions. No, the purpose is to demonstrate that tutorials can be interwoven into a game in as non-invasive a manner as possible, obeying all of the principles we have seen throughout this book, and still teach players how to have a great time playing the game. After finishing this document and some mockups, I hope you will have a sense of how you can take some of the stuff you have read here and apply it to your own games at your company or in your garage. Just in case you don't, the final chapter has a bullet point list of all of the things you can do to your own game prototypes based on the things you have learned. So, without further ado, let me introduce our game.

Figure 7.1 *Escape from Skull Island* title card. (Figure courtesy of Peter Kalmar.)

Escape from Skull Island

Escape from Skull Island is a two-dimensional isometric action RPG, not unlike many of the most popular role-playing games of the *Super Nintendo* era (see Figure 7.1). The game takes place on a horrific island inhabited by a mad scientist where a group of adventurers has been convinced a vast treasure is hidden. Unfortunately for our hapless heroes, *Dr. Horrordoom* has riddled the island with traps, monsters, and an uncanny sense of existential angst. It will be up to our ragtag band of heroes to solve puzzles, fight monsters, allocate skill points, delve through a randomly generated dungeon, and *Escape from Skull Island* alive!

Overview of Mechanics and Gameplay

Escape from Skull Island is first and foremost an action role-playing game with rogue-like and dungeon-crawling elements. Players will be able to select a party of three from a list of six available characters, and will be placed in the depths of the dungeon, whereupon they will discover the treasure is a lie, the setup was a trap, and they now have to navigate their way out of the maze while *Dr. Horrordoom* tries to do them in. Each of six characters matches an associated role-playing game archetype. These are warrior, barbarian, mage, cleric, rogue, and paladin, although they are amusingly themed from archaeologist to ballerina to basketball player. Because this is a set-up for a book and not an actual design document, I'll spare you the details of how all of this happens. Suffice to say each one behaves as you think they might. Of course, from your reading, you should now know that assuming that players will know what these classes are is a mistake, and assuming that players will know how they play is also a mistake. For this reason, we are going to design learning experiences for them that are endogenous, non-threatening, and stay in accordance with all of the tutorials we have seen throughout the book.

After selecting their three characters, players begin the game by pressing a begin button. Play is in real time, similar to contemporary dungeon-crawling titles. Players will encounter enemies who will attack them on-sight in various ways with projectile, melee, and magic attacks. When a member of the party dies, they are dead and out of the game. When the party is wiped out, the game is over (see Figure 7.2). To this end, the game is a hard-as-nails type rogue-like, but still an action role-playing game, as enemies do not "wait" for the player to act. Of course, players are going to have no idea what I mean by ARPG or rogue-like, so we are going to create learning so that even if they don't know anything, they can still have a great time.

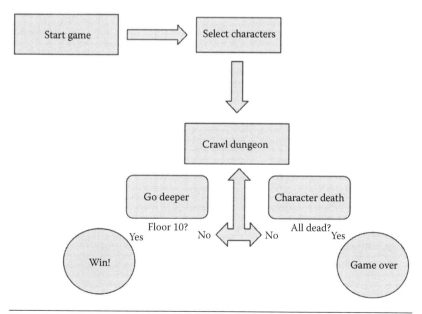

Figure 7.2 *Skull Island* flow chart. (Screenshot courtesy of Matthew White.)

The player initially starts the game as the first character he or she chose, but can switch between them by pressing the Z or X buttons to cycle counterclockwise and clockwise, respectively. Consistent with auditory cueing, a sound similar to a flipping page is heard when players switch characters, and the current character is centered in the camera. Players can collect items to equip that will increase their stats. I will show you how we will teach the players this in a little bit. The stats are simple: health, damage, and defense. I know it is not complicated and won't sell, but hey, I'm not actually making the game! For the purposes of demonstrating a tutorial, this is easy. Leveling up increases statistics in different ways depending on which class you choose. Clerics and paladins cannot attack but can heal. The objective is to crawl out of the dungeon alive across 10 randomly generated floors without being killed. If I have time, I will release 30 or so DLC packs to change the appearance of the characters. No, I probably won't.

Controls and Inputs Overview

Escape from Skull Island is a mouse and keyboard game. That said, players use W, A, S, and D to move their characters, the left mouse button to attack enemies and open doors or chests, the right click to pick things up, and the tab key to open their inventory, which they may manipulate with left clicks of the mouse. This is pretty much it for controls for *Skull Island*. Players will be instructed in how to manipulate their characters with in-line tutorials that do not interrupt gameplay, and that are consistent with the things I have discussed in this book.

Interface Structure and Overview

The interface is very thin and simple (see Figure 7.3). Players have a health indicator underneath their players consistent with the contiguity principle discussed in Chapter 6. This health bar doesn't show up until the characters are hurt. In an effort to reduce cognitive load, we are trying to keep things that players need to know as close to their gaze as possible, and keep clutter off the screen. Eye tracking will tell us that players have a "center-screen" habit, and will tend to look

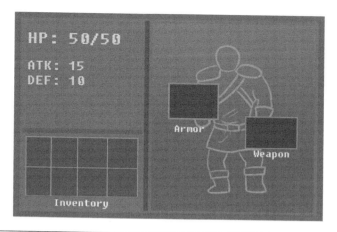

Figure 7.3 Inventory overlay. (Figure courtesy of Peter Kalmar.)

in the center of their vision in the absence of novel things to look at. For this reason, the camera follows the selected player, and the health bar is in-game just below the character. Play pauses while characters manage their inventory. The inventory screen is opened by pressing TAB. Once players are in the inventory screen, they can equip items in two slots: *Armor* and *Weapon*. On the left side of the screen rests the player's statistics. On the right side is the equipment paper-doll that illustrates where things go.

Tutorials and Learning in Escape from Skull Island

This is where we get to the meat of the application. We are going to assume nothing about our player base. As far as I'm concerned, *Escape from Skull Island* is the first and only game my audience has ever played, or will ever play. It is incorrect, most likely, but that assumption will force me to discard everything about games that I have learned over years of playing and making them. If it helps you to remember this point, imagine that the games you are making are being designed to be used in SETI (search for extraterrestrial intelligence). Barring the language, of course, anyone (or anything) should be able to understand your game and accomplish the objectives. Doing the opposite is what we call an exclusionary behavior. We have been over these in the previous chapters, and they are undesirable in almost every circumstance. When we forcibly exclude some people, we often paint with a broader stroke than we intend and alienate our audience. Learning in the game starts from the moment it is turned on. We are going to go ahead and talk about each portion of the game in sequence—boot, main menu and save/load functions, begin game screen, gameplay and advancement, and the Game Over screen.

Learning at Boot

As long as players are breathing, they are learning something. For this reason, let's assume that they are indeed breathing when the game is booting. If you inundate them with your company's logo screen, a startup video, a technology video screen indicating the type of audio codec you used in the game, and a logo screen from your parent corporation, they've already learned something: in this game, I have to wait to have fun. So, for this reason, the first thing someone booting *Escape from Skull Island* is going to see is the main menu. Boot will be so thin you will think there is something wrong. Like the first time you turned your computer on after having installed a solid-state hard drive, you will simply feel like games aren't supposed to start this fast. It will be like going out and getting married before you even start dating. It will be like wanting a cookie and having it appear on your desk. It will be like… okay, you get the point… fast.

Why am I going to do this? Well, it is simple. Players expect to play. When they turn the game on, they should get what they expect. Imagine for a moment that you are playing hopscotch for the first time. Instead of walking around and looking at the chalk on the ground, you are chained to a desk and not allowed to stand up or look at the playfield until the person who drew the chalk on the ground tells you all about how he drew it, how proud he is of it, and how he used the most cutting-edge chalk available, and then tells you that you are going to get to see it after he explains it to you some more. Not very natural, right? Almost seems like you are being held prisoner. Well, that is exactly what you are doing in a game; you are taking the player's cognition prisoner. The result is not positive. In the event that your company forces you to display a startup screen, it should be less than one second in length and any input should skip it. If you are an indie game company and think that displaying a company logo and a tech logo at startup will make you feel more "official," skip it. You should take input during a cut scene or logo as a clear message: I don't care about this, why is nothing happening? After boot, presumably the first thing the player will see is the game's main menu in almost every game project. Naturally, *Skull Island* follows this pattern.

Mindfulness at the Main Menu

The main menu is the gateway to your game. Have you ever seen a well-designed amusement park or subway station? Where you need to go is obvious and, ideally, inviting. If your game is complex enough that it needs a separate tutorial menu option, then that is going to be the second menu option. They should appear in this order: CONTINUE, TUTORIAL, NEW GAME, OPTIONS. Anyone who works in design outside of the games industry will know that things are often ordered by the amount they are to be used. Ever notice that your turn signal in your car is easier to access than your four-way or hazard lights? There is a reason for that. Notice that your gearshift is more accessible than the lever to pop your hood? There is a reason for that, too. If we go back to our principle about assuming nothing about our players, it is entirely possible that they don't even know how to navigate the menu. For this reason, burying the tutorial three layers deep inside of DLC and extras is a bad idea.

The main menu itself is going to teach our players. We are going to model movement through the menu options with a subtle cue. We will assume that there are *bone minions* wandering around in *Escape from Skull Island*. One of those minions is going to walk in front of the menu options in a parallax effect, and throw bones at the menu options. The options will smack and crack as he hits them with projectiles, and then saunters off the screen. Why does this matter? Well, we learned in Chapter 3 that the cognitive apprenticeship principle of modeling makes us want to do things that another person has done. In this case, without telling the player, the minion has indicated that the menu options are interactive. When things touch these, something happens. Unfortunately, in keeping with our earlier principles of cognitive load, we can't put something on the screen that says, "Hey press WASD to move through menu options." For this reason, I am going to make any input other than WASD select the currently highlighted menu option. Why should the player have to dig through the keyboard commands? I am also going to make W, A, S, and D, as well as the arrow keys, move through the menus. When all else fails, the player will look to the keyboard for guidance, and there are no clearer buttons on the keyboard than the arrows.

The continue screen is simply going to show the files to load, as you might expect. Players will be able to load a file by pressing any input other than the arrow keys, or W, A, S, D. The game will autosave for the players and doesn't need to show them the autosave notice. It is outdated, and hardware saves so blindingly fast and has such space these days, there is no reason to show that notice anymore. Once players hit the button to load the game, the loading icon will be in line, with no separate loading screen. This isn't 1997; games don't take more than a few seconds to load anymore. The notable exception here should be when your game is enormous and has a lengthy install, or harsh loading times, which of course is something that should be fixed anyway. Attention is often time-limited, as we have talked about throughout the book, and every moment the player isn't playing or doing something entertaining, you are losing him or her.

Designing an Excellent Character Select Screen

I am sure many of you have at some point in your career designed a character select screen. In *Escape from Skull Island*, the player is able to pick three party members. Two of them will be played by artificial intelligence when they are not controlled by the player. To this end, a character select screen will allow the player to cycle between different characters and add them to his or her party before beginning the game (see Figure 7.4).

Consistent with our contiguity principle from Chapter 6, all of the information is located in the correct place to minimize cognitive load on the player while selecting characters. The Z and X buttons move the character selection between characters, while the C button adds the character to the party. If the player doesn't add a character for more than 30 seconds, any button other than Z and X will add the character to the party. Once the player has selected three party members, the game starts. You will notice the placement of the Z and X buttons in the image. When the player presses Z or X, the sound of a flipping page is heard, and a new character is highlighted in the selection area. The character's name is displayed. Once the character has been

Figure 7.4 Character selection screen. (Figure courtesy of Peter Kalmar.)

selected, he or she no longer appears in the selections, and is instead present as an animated face inside the party selector box at the bottom of the screen. Note that the Z and X buttons are to the left and right of the character on-screen, reminiscent of flipping a page. This level of cognitive proximity will make the interface feel natural, and not incur additional extraneous cognitive load. This is again consistent with the contiguity principle.

Because we know that learners learn better from speech than from text alone, narrations regarding the character's particular skills are added here. They are *not* displayed on screen as text, consistent with the redundancy principle. Rather, players are shown an animation on the right side, with its volume significantly reduced, while a narration in character, consistent with the personalization principle, tells the player about the character's particular abilities. Consider the following narration:

> Walt Smith, the Archaeologist, is a rash and debonair character. Equipped with a gun, he rushes into battle and can attack enemies from a distance. He is not very strong, and is easily toppled, but is very useful in the right party. Walt has moderate health with low defense.

Sure, this could have been displayed more simply as on-screen text, but as we have seen, players often ignore prolific on-screen text in order to get to the playing portion of the game. It is difficult to penalize them for skipping it because there is no meaningful way to do so.

This is one of the many beautiful parts about using voice-overs and audio learning. If the player decides to switch characters before the voice-over finishes, we are going to gently scold them. Observe the following narration that happens if the player decides to press Z or X while the narrator is talking:

> Oh, impatient are we? Okay, I'll just talk about this next character...

The gentle prod is a method we use in teaching all the time. As I have said throughout the book, it is important that players realize that they have done something they are not supposed to, but not be punished brutally early on. This gentle chastising at the hands of the game's narrator is humorous, and keeps them on task to listen to the game's instructions about how to use the character. On the flip side, we don't want experienced players to be babied, so if the player skips by switching characters or adds characters to his or her party before the narrator finishes the discussion a second time, the following narration takes place:

> Well, fine then. I'll just be over here. Press TAB if you need me.

An image labeled "Help: TAB" appears in the bottom right of the screen. The game saves this preference to a file so that experienced players don't have to fight with it every time they start the game, incurring extraneous additional cognitive load for no particular reason. On the other hand, in the unlikely event that a novice player accidentally mashes his or her way through canceling the narrator, the player has the option to bring him back.

In addition to the principles I have listed thus far, the multimedia principle is also strong here. Like many new tutorials are adopting, an animation of the character using his or her skills is apparent on the right side of the screen. The narrator begins to talk as this animation begins to play, so due to cognitive proximity, it is very likely that the player will watch the animation while listening to the narrator. Not only does this serve as a structured function for sound that holds attention, it also is consistent with our conversation about modeling in the cognitive apprenticeship model of teaching. The NPC in the animation serves as an expert, who is performing duties that the player needs to emulate. This emulation learning is step one in scaffolding, where the emulation is complete—a type of worked example—and then is gradually pulled away to let the player take over. In fact, considering the game makes use of AI players, this animation could be real time to make sure players get the idea that this really happens in the game.

The character select screen does not overly prompt the player, as is common in current games. Instead of giving extra cognitive load with a lot of on-screen commands to read, sift through, and try to understand, once the third character has been selected, a simple "Begin game?" prompt appears in the middle of the screen, graying out the background, silencing all sound, and sending a loud drum effect to draw the player's attention. If the player presses no (X), he or she is brought back to the beginning of the character select screen with an empty party. If the player selects yes (any other button), the game begins.

The Game Screen

I hope that this is where most of our actual learning will take place. As I am sure you have read throughout the book by this point, good learning in games is a combination of smart tutorial design through well-implemented instruction and well-constructed levels, as well as constant and clear feedback. Well, there is no better game to provide feedback than *Escape from Skull Island*. Why is that, you might ask? Well, here are a few key points.

- Multiple NPC characters means death isn't a vicious, horrific punishment. You could still survive with only one character intact. This allows players to fail without being harshly punished at first.
- AI are programmed to attack enemies, seek health, and hide in cover when they are overwhelmed. This means a player who hasn't played yet can observe expert behavior early on in order to emulate it.
- Numerous party members means numerous sources of information with distinct auditory voices. This means the players will not have the action interrupted while being told how to play.

Isn't it neat how design objectives wrap so nicely into learning objectives? Well, I think it's neat, anyway. This is going to persist throughout the entirety of gameplay. Death is a learning experience, not because we wait until players have died to give them hints, but because the methods of their demise are indicators of bad performance.

When players begin the game in *Escape from Skull Island*, they are presented with a short in-game scene of the chosen party members opening the cryptic chest of existential woe at the center of the island where the treasure was rumored to have been stored. Instead, they are greeted by the holographic visage of *Dr. Horrordoom*, telling them that they are prey in his grand scheme, and he has unleashed a horde of monsters, traps, and other deadly things to do them in. His intention, of course, is to use their lifeless, mangled bodies in a bizarre marionette show to entertain his mutant pet lemur, *Hans*. In order to prevent this Lovecraftian nightmare, the heroes must escape, and they must do so by using the WASD keys to navigate—gaining levels, getting more powerful, equipping better items, and getting off the island in one piece. Unfortunately for them, an explosion goes off at the very moment the recording ends, with *Dr. Horrordoom* cackling maniacally in the background.

The first thing players are greeted with after the smoke settles is the shouting of one of their party members. The shouting uses three-dimensional sound to indicate the direction from which the sound is emanating. Consider the following dialog:

Hey! (Player's chosen character's name)! I'm over here! *hack... cough*... Some of the rubble fell on top of me and I can't move... can you walk?

If you thought that this is where we are going to put a pop-up that says "OMG PRESS WASD TO MOVE," you thought wrong. We already have almost all of our cognitive resources for visual stuff used up; look at the screenshot in Figure 7.5.

Let's do some math. There is a compass in the top right corner that orients the player in 3D space; we will call this one unit of cognitive resource. On top of that is the layout of the dungeon itself, demarcated with things like rubble, doors, spatial dimensions, and so on. For the sake of brevity, we will call those two additional units of cognitive load. The player is unharmed, so his or her health bar is not yet visible. There is an enemy on screen; we will call that one more. There is also an NPC ally, which is one more. Assuming the player notices

Figure 7.5 In-game screenshot. (Figure courtesy of Peter Kalmar.)

the exit door in the top right and hears the off-screen murmurs of the trapped ally as described above, we're up to seven. That is about as tight as I can possibly run this ship without causing the player to lose his or her mind and throw the keyboard out the window.

Keep in mind that all of the information (for the most part) here is visual. For that reason, we can offload some of the cognitive load to the auditory channel instead of bogging down the visual. In addition, this is a great place for us to offer learning support. The player has already received a prompt to move around:

... Some of the rubble fell on top of me and I can't move... can you walk?

The player is compelled to act. The character has been requested to help an ally who has, apparently, been trapped by rubble. Assuming the player doesn't know that WASD is the default movement for most PC games, he or she will probably start mashing buttons. When the player presses the wrong ones, like ZXVC, or the arrow keys, we are going to move him or her anyway. The movement will be staggered, as if the player were injured by the explosion. The ally will chime in:

No... no that's not right. You're close... try a little harder to get your footing ... use the WASD keys to steady yourself and move!

In this way, we wait for players to fail before we inundate them with tutorials they might not actually need. If players have pre-existing knowledge on how to play PC games, they will likely go for the

WASD keys anyway, at which point we can assume they are experts and never show them that particular bit of tutorial information.

The next bit of tutorial learning is presented in the enemies that are on screen. *Bone Minions*, the default enemy in our lovely menagerie, are present and visible, and they are approaching the party. This should cause some trepidation in the player; however, without the player's knowledge, the enemies will deprioritize the selected character (e.g., the player) until the player has personally killed one. This dynamic difficulty adjustment means that the enemies are going to target AI players much more frequently than human ones until the player learns the ropes. This will continue throughout the game. This test-retest of player competency allows the game to keep track of the player's skill level. For example, if the player kills 5 out of 10 enemies on a floor, and the AI kill the other 5, it is safe to say the player is doing well. If the player kills 0, on the other hand, it is safe to say the player needs to continue to experiment. These kinds of rich data hooks allow us to subtly and dynamically render new challenges and learning objectives for our players.

In addition to keeping players interested, keeping dungeons randomly generated stays consistent with Dewey's ideas of experience. Players cannot automatize the dungeon (as easily) as they could if the experience were pre-rendered. This is standard in dungeon-crawling games and is one of the key appeals. The theme of procedurally rendered rewards and punishments should be clear here. Every time the player performs a good behavior in *Escape from Skull Island*, such as picking up a treasure, gaining a level, slaying an enemy, or engaging in combat, the music is dynamically rendered to increase in its tempo and timbre to add to the gravity of the situation. This is called a procedurally generated reward, and is a great way to promote a flow experience by doing some of the things we spoke about regarding flow in the previous chapter. The musical cues provide clear feedback, while the increasing and dynamically generated nature of the rewards maintains balance between skill level and appropriate rewards. Presenting this feedback via the auditory channel continues to manage cognitive load responsibly while simultaneously providing feedback.

Similarly, the punishments are dynamically generated. Players are presented with a jarring loss of music when hit. The music will change its timbre from one of upbeat amazing epic, to one of downtrodden, boring, and silent. Eventually after being beaten enough or losing enough characters, the music will stop altogether. Remembering to make clever use of sound, the players will associate silence with poor performance and wide sweeping orchestral pieces with positive performance. This paves a reward pathway for us to use. Just like the musical cues in older games stuck with you as an indicator of gaining a life, finding a secret, or winning a battle, the musical cues in *Skull Island* will keep the player engaged and on task.

Audio cues are used in a few other ways to enhance learning. When enemies emerge onto the screen, an orchestral hit from that direction cues their appearance. Treasure dropping is met with the sound of objects hitting the floor and twinkling, so to speak. A visual cue accompanies the auditory cue, as the treasure glows slightly. This is consistent with the multimedia principle, as well as the attentional control theory that tells us that consistent and clear uses of sound will be more memorable than ad-libbed or stochastic ones. Programming hooks are included that detect when a player has not moved, been hit repeatedly, is repeatedly missing the target, cannot find the exit, leaves items on the ground, or performs other problematic behaviors. Auditory instructions without on-screen text, consistent with the redundancy principle, teach the player how to cull those behaviors and quiet the music when the AI is speaking, activating the same reward pathway established through music earlier: less music means worse performance, ergo, the tips will be context relevant. It is important to determine what these undesired behaviors would be early in your game projects so you can address what kinds of tutorial tips and help will be necessary to guide players through. A good way to determine this is to look at level and mechanic designs and ask yourself, "What is the exact opposite of what I would like the player to do here?"

Auditory cues from the AI players also provide dynamic feedback on all of the actions the player takes. The odd "Nice shot!" or what have you provides feedback that the player has successfully attacked an enemy. These auditory tips become more infrequent as the game progresses so as not to overload the player. When players equip a piece of armor or weapon, they are greeted with inclusive praise from their AI compatriots: "Whoa... cool gun!" or "That armor looks sturdy." On the other hand, when they equip a lower-level item, they are greeted with the opposite: "I'm not so sure that fits you quite right..."

or "That gun looks a little worn out..." Positive reinforcement fades and becomes random; that is, it happens some of the time, but not all of the time. On the other hand, negative reactions stay constant to attempt to correct the player behavior by quieting the music and providing the player auditory feedback.

As players gain levels, auditory cues indicate this to them, and other players will instruct them, verbally, as to how to open the menu and distribute skill points. A combination of on-screen glow effects and dictated instructions will guide players through the process of allocating skill points. Taken together, this auditory learning, coupled with the tips presented to the player in the form of dynamically increased difficulty, AI programming, procedurally rendered music, and constant and amazing rewards, will keep the players engaged without cognitively overloading them.

Learning from Loss: The Game Over Screen

The last portion of *Skull Island*, my indie megahit, which I will describe here, is the Game Over screen. This is a familiar fixture of games dating back as far as any of us can likely remember, and is a great indicator that one has failed. To that end, it is a type of formative punishment. We want players to realize that their undesirable behaviors have led them to this conclusion, but a few things need to be constant.

First, Game Over screens should not be fun. Do not put mini games on them, or funny quips. Do not give the player something awesome for dying, like a mega amazing assault rifle that makes the next time easier. Do not offer a chance to skip a level. Do not provide tutorial hints once the players have died. Remember the behavioral effect we discussed in Chapter 3: when players execute a behavior, the type of feedback they receive within a few seconds dictates whether they continue or extinguish that behavior. If it is your intention to make sure players keep dying intentionally, make the Game Over screen a blitz of amazing awesomeness, pepper it with hints and tips, or give them something fun. The result is players who want to die. Instead, make the Game Over screen an eldritch horror. If the game is lively and colorful, make the Game Over screen black as night. If fun jaunty music is playing, try jarring silence. Make cacophonous horrible noises. Seriously, just play a vacuum cleaner mixed with a blender grinding up a glass jar full of pennies. Players should very nearly hate seeing this screen!

None of this is to say that you shouldn't give players an option to skip sequences, give them amazing weapons to give them an easier time, provide them tips, or entertain them. However, I hope we have learned that *what* we teach is exactly as important as *when* we teach it. We want to offer players rewards when they have done something that we want them to do, such as accessing a menu, navigating a level, or overcoming an obstacle, so as to reinforce those behaviors. If instead we reward them at the Game Over screen, that is going to have unintended effects.

To this end, the Game Over screen in *Skull Island* is as classic as you might expect. The game cues down its orchestral soundtrack to a slow, dull hum, until it eventually is replaced with total silence and the sound of *Dr. Horrordoom* cackling. This cackling sounds awful. It is loud, ugly, and jarring. It is punctuated with lightning blasts and the sound of the island collapsing with a backdrop of pure black, fading to bright, blinding red. The words GAME OVER are emblazoned across the screen in white, contrasting harshly with the background. Players are held on this screen for 5 seconds, after which any input will return them to the main menu. This screen is very clearly and without a doubt a punishment. There is a catch: if players die on the first floor, they are instead simply returned to the main menu. Remember that we only want to punish players after we know they can win. If players feel like they are being blindsided by punishments, they will stop playing. So, to that end, we use the same mechanics for detecting player behavior that we used in the gameplay example to determine when or when not to show the Game Over screen.

Summary

This chapter takes most of what I have talked about in the book and makes it into a nice cohesive package. As such, I haven't really introduced any new information, so there is no cheat sheet. What I would like you to take away from this chapter is that there is a place in game design for understanding how the mind assimilates information.

Another thing I would like you to take away is that many of the psychological principles in the book line up nicely with game design. As a result, many of the changes we can make to our games to line them up more correctly with human cognitive structures are not substantial, but can have an enormous impact. In the following chapter, I am going to review every bit of material we have covered in the book with specific reference to implementation in your game projects. I hope it will be useful for you!

8
BULLET POINT
LEARNING DESIGN

If you really wanted to, you could tear out this portion of the book and staple it to your office wall. This portion of the book is usable, popular, and referential. I recognize that game developers have a lot of creativity and drive, but very little time to sit down and read a book cover to cover. Driving home the read-and-use approach taken by this book, this chapter is a blow-by-blow list of bullet points about designing learning for games that has been wrought through years of research and game design. Designers can take these and put them directly into game projects to improve the engagement, retention, and enjoyment experienced by their players. Hopefully, this chapter can take your knowledge from this book with you to your next game project.

There Are Really Three Things

You have probably noticed that I have abandoned the word *tutorial* as part of the title of this chapter, and there is a reason for that. I hope that throughout the book you have realized that you are building more than just tutorials, but rather, you are building learning mechanics that teach people to play. While this is by no means an authoritative statement, I'd like to call that learning design. I have borrowed a lot from multimedia learning theories and research in my own work, and throughout the book I have used a lot of the evidence from those studies to justify my design principles. There are really three concrete categories into which all of these design principles and rules fall. I hope throughout the book you have disabused yourself of the myth that all tutorials are mandatory, unskippable, torturous exercises in misery. The research I have been conducting over the last few years suggests that three mechanics-based approaches work particularly well in getting people to learn from your game, which ideally aids in encouraging flow and, of course, keeps people playing.

1. Make sure all players are able to reach the same skill level very quickly.
2. Reward success and punish failure quickly, harshly, and overtly.
3. Do not ignore the wealth of data at your fingertips.

Each of these can be further broken down into the points we have covered in this book. Therefore, without further rambling, here is the list that you may tear out and glue to your wall (make sure it is your own wall; I claim no legal responsibility for your actions).

Three Principles of Learning Design

1. Make sure *all* players reach the same skill level quickly.
   - No exclusionary mechanics.
   - No "club" behaviors.
   - Offer learning support.
   - Follow the cognitive principles.
   - Let skilled players be skillful as fast as possible.
   - Reward failures.
2. Reward success and punish mistakes quickly, harshly, and overtly.
   - No small punishments (*except early on*).
   - No small rewards (*ever!*).
   - Immediate feedback on all inputs.
   - Massive explosions of juiciness.
   - Harsh and brutal correction of unwanted behaviors.
   - Rewards must scale in their splendor and awesomeness.
3. Do not ignore the wealth of data at your fingertips.
   - Dynamic difficulty adjustment.
   - Test/retest player skill level.
   - Use just-in-time tactics to reward continued play.
   - Procedural and dynamic rewards and punishments.
   - You cannot have too many data-collection hooks.

These should all be easy to understand. We have gone over just about all of them in the book at some point or another. I am going to go over some things here in summary, using the bullets above as talking points to link your learning back to other things you have read in the book.

No Exclusionary Mechanics

Why this rule? Well, you have learned throughout the book that one of the most important keys to good learning is feedback. Feedback is used in promoting flow experiences, and is important to either cultivate or remove behaviors if they are wanted or unwanted, respectively. Exclusionary mechanics are elements of a game that make it intentionally unapproachable. I'm not suggesting that games like this aren't profitable, awesome, or valuable. What I'm suggesting is that if your goal is to reach the broadest market possible and have people from all walks of life enjoy playing your game, certain mechanics will make this more difficult. Exclusionary mechanics include extreme initial learning curves, needless complexity, incredibly math-heavy mechanics, and wildly abstract mechanics like changing control schemes or inconsistent feedback. Again, if your intention is to create a game that appeals to a very small segment of the population, go for it! However, if your goal were widespread adoption and enjoyment, I would personally avoid these cognitive-load heavy juggernauts.

No "Club" Behaviors

We talked about this a lot in Chapter 2. A club or clique behavior is one that intentionally pits groups of users against other groups of users. In some multiplayer scenarios, this is desirable. Think *World of Warcraft*, for example—two warring factions locked in brutal combat for the same land makes sense and frames the narrative for that game. On the other hand, if you are to create things like character levels in multiplayer, they should be achievable by different metrics. Let me explain—if you are about to play a game of, say, *League of Legends*, but can't get anyone to join your queue because you're not the maximum level, the likelihood of you continuing to play is going to suffer if you're an average player. On the other hand, if you are one of the players in the "club," hey, your day is going to be great. *League* does a great job of mitigating this eventuality with multiplayer games by offering different game modes, different levels of play, numerous champions, and more. The principle that ought to be avoided remains the same—being excluded feels bad, and will discourage new players from entering the experience. How you will implement this will differ from project to project, but a good indicator is this: if you see a club forming and, more importantly, if you see a group of excluded people forming, something is going wrong.

Offer Learning Support

This might as well be the title of the book. If learners can't figure out how to engage with your game before they reach their frustration or boredom threshold, they're not going to play. Learning support comes in all forms, and in my opinion based on research and game design experience, I'd say that cognitive apprenticeship offers the best structure and set of instructional design strategies for learning in games. I talk about that throughout the book. You should always offer some kind of expert behavior for the players to model. The easiest way to get this in without it feeling artificial is through an NPC. You should always offer optional help if the player needs to look it up. Where possible, mandatory help should be done with sound rather than text. Through proper learning support, we attempt to minimize cognitive load so that learners can emphasize learning to play over having to parse redundant information. If you really are keen on offering amazing learning support to your players, please read the Appendix for information on further reading that will make you a better teacher and, I hope, a happier game designer.

Follow the Cognitive Principles

As much as we like to deny it sometimes, there is a huge amount in common between movies, short films, training videos, and games. They all share one particular thing: they simultaneously present information via audio and video to a user—often a single user. This similarity means that much of the research done on all these other forms of media has an application here as well. Future research needs to demonstrate exactly how the cognitive principles affect game design, which is what I am currently heavily invested in doing—job security and the like. If anything, we should note that the cognitive space required for games is in fact greater than it is for films and other forms of audiovisual media. This is because the learners have to actively solve puzzles or overcome obstacles of some kind in order to advance. Because of this, the amount of cognitive load left over to parse through instructions is very limited. To that end, we owe it to our players to mitigate cognitive load to the greatest extent possible. The easiest way to implement this without years of education in cognitive psychology, in my opinion, is to implement Mayer's Cognitive Principles into our game design mechanics as much as possible. Surely, they have to be adapted to game-like displays—some of the things that Mayer wrote don't give themselves easily to games. On the other hand, elements like the contiguity principle make perfect sense to interface and game design. We talked about this in Chapter 6, so feel free to go back there for more explanation, or check out the further reading in the Appendix.

Let Skilled Players Be Skillful as Fast as Possible

There is definitely a demographic of your audience that is not going to appreciate being taught how to walk over and over again. It is extremely important that you let them get to being amazing as quick as possible. So to that end, it is very important that you detect skilled play as fast as possible. In Chapter 7, we talked about a way to teach the players to use the keys (WASD) to walk around. This was simple; you just took any input as wobbly walking, corrected them with audio cues until they put their hands on WASD, and then continued. The logical counter to detecting unskilled play is detecting when players do things right and making sure to scaffold back your teaching appropriately. How do we do that? Well, in our *Skull Island* example, we could detect whether the players needed to be corrected in how to walk, or if they naturally put their hands on WASD. People aren't intrinsically aware that WASD makes characters move—they had to learn it somewhere. In this sense, using WASD indicates a level of skill. A typist lays his or her hands on the home row keys (e.g., A S D F J K L ; SPACE), whereas a gamer lays his her hands on the keys most notably associated with gaming (e.g., W A S D SPACE SHIFT). Don't believe me? Look at your keyboard. My WASD letters are literally worn off. What this tells the program is if players use WASD to move without prompting, suppress the moving tutorial. If players attack an enemy without first taking a hit, suppress the attacking tutorial. This is extremely important in managing cognitive load. Learners who are already skilled face the expertise-reversal effect of having instruction actually increase their cognitive load instead of decreasing it. To avoid this, we need to detect player success as well as failure, and rescind our teaching accordingly. This lets our skilled players be skilled immediately.

Reward Failures

This seems at odds with other things I have told you in this book. I want to clarify what I mean by a certain type of failure as opposed to unwanted behavior. The failure we want to reward is the failure that occurs when we attempt to do something for the first time, or with very little training, and do it poorly. This should be rewarded because we tried, and to some extent hopefully learned something. On the other hand, an unwanted behavior is something like being unable to dodge bullets, return fire, use the cover mechanic, manage the inventory, and so on, after having previously done it successfully. In order to execute any punishment, we have to be sure that our learners have learned how to perform the task. For example, it is useless to punish an infant for babbling. They are trying to talk, and if you want to encourage talking, you have to give them what I like to call corrective rewards. This takes something that needs to be corrected, like babbling, and removes it while still encouraging the core of what the baby is trying to do—talk. A corrective reward for this kind of thing might be the baby looking at a bottle and saying *babbsbdbsdbpppgth!*, to which I will reply, "Yes, BOTT - LE. B O TT L E," after which I will give the baby the bottle. I have made a clear and present correction by enforcing the word *bottle* repeatedly and distancing the request from the reward, but haven't relinquished the reward entirely, merely delayed it. In *Skull Island*, we did this by making the AI prioritize AI targets until the player makes his or her first kill. This way, the player will not be targeted for lack of knowledge, and will still be able to make the mistake of dying (via his or her AI partner). The training wheels come off once the player has demonstrated mastery by killing a monster. There are subtle ways to reward correctively in most any game.

No Small Punishments

Death should mean something. I played a student game recently where all of the tutorials, hints, controls—everything—were shown after you died. Not only is this completely backward in terms of learning, game design, whatever, it also makes death completely meaningless. If you are actually meta-gaming to die intentionally so that you get your hands on the tips, it means first that there is not enough information being presented to you, and second that death is meaningless. Once players have learned a topic, they reify their knowledge through skill and drill, which is a facet of behaviorism that we talked about in Chapter 3 and elsewhere. Once a student has something down, he or she repeats it. As long as the results continue to be good, the behavior becomes automatized, at which point the cognitive load required to do it significantly decreases. If you have ever wondered why people who play competitive games are able to track hundreds of interactions per minute, or why healers in MMORPGS can focus on parties of dozens of people simultaneously, this is the answer.

What is happening in the brains of players when punishments are small or trivial is likely the opposite of what the developers wanted. If death means nothing, players are likely either automatizing it as a means to an end and will intentionally die, as in the student example, or it is just irritating them. If you are irritating the player as a punishment, you had better be sure that the punishment is short and immediate. If the punishment doesn't affect the player's ability to win the game, but rather just wastes his or her time, the player is going to resent the game for that. Again, players are coming to a game in search of a leisurely, enjoyable experience. If you betray that desire with constant arbitrary punishment, they will just put the game down. For this reason, your consequences must be harsh. Want to drop players to the last checkpoint when they die? How about dropping all of their items, too? There is no such thing as being too harsh once you have taught them how to play the game. The mistake my students often make is introducing this harsh atmosphere much too early, and instead of motivating players to cull all of their undesirable behaviors, they just incentivize them to put the controller down.

No Small Rewards

This one really baffles me. One of the strongest contributors to learning is getting amazing feedback in such a way that you have a great time, or an explosion of awesomeness immediately after a desired behavior. This should be amazingly easy in games; after all, games are designed to make people have a good time! Unfortunately, we sometimes dole rewards out bit by bit. We will show the players a badass amazing character early on that they're intended to emulate, but then make them play the entire game to get to that point. Worse still, we sometimes let the character play that badass version of themselves, then artificially strip their power away, making them effectively play the entire game to get back to the power level they had at the beginning of the game. Why not let the players emulate that character and then surpass them? This was the norm in older games, but we have stopped for some reason. If you have ever played *Saints Row IV*, it is likely that you are familiar with constant amazing rewards. The game literally dumps rewards in your lap repeatedly and continuously throughout the experience—and that's amazing.

We know from what we have been reading that there are only two things you can do with a behavior—reinforce it or correct it. If the desired behavior is to be able to jump over obstacles, there should be rollercoasters, fireworks, T-bone steaks, and fine cigars on the other side. Other game designers have called a cascade of amazing things that happen after minor input *juiciness*, and I think that is an appropriate enough term. Juicy games are ones that give the players huge experiences without requiring them to do much in way of input. This doesn't mean you are going to spoil the player: there's no such thing! There is no shortage of good things you can do for the player. It's not like if you give them a bajillion dollars and a ton of amazing weapons after the first mission you will run out of amazing experiences to give them, as if fun is a finite resource. For this reason, and to continue reinforcing good behavior, including overcoming obstacles and playing your game, you have to make certain that rewards are ample and continuous.

Immediate Feedback on All Inputs

It is generally accepted that in order for a behavioral lesson to work, you need to either reinforce or correct a behavior within about 3 seconds of it happening. That might even be too large a window for games. I will go ahead and say that for games, anything more than 1 second is too long. I will fall back on the dog training analogy: when the dog does something good, you pet him, praise him, or give him a treat immediately. On the other hand, if you don't catch him in the act of pooping in your bed, there's no point in punishing him. He has already lost the cognitive trace. This is especially true of games. Players have to connect something they have done with something that happened in the game. The best way to make certain this link is not broken is with temporal proximity, as we discussed in Chapter 3. In games, this means making sure that victories are rewarded instantly and shortcomings are punished equally rapidly. After time, this will cause the player to associate the behavior in-game with the outcome. For example, if dying causes players to lose their money after being shown a Game Over screen, they will eventually associate dying with losing money, and omit the Game Over screen as a cognitive middleman. If you just cause them to lose their money immediately the second they die, they will make that association much more quickly. In order to make sure players want to keep playing, rewards and punishments need to be instant, or at least very soon after the behavior.

Massive Explosions of Juiciness

Juiciness is a term that comes up a lot in my teaching. As I have talked about in a few chapters in this book, it boils down to small input, big output. If you can push a button and all kinds of amazing things happen on the screen, go for it. You will find in life that when you attempt similar things, like martial arts for example, actually performing the action in question takes much more effort than just pressing a button. This is one of the magical things about games. Consistent with Dewey's talk on experiences that we covered in Chapter 3, it is important to know that players want an experience instead of just experience points. Through juicy interactions, we can make this possible. Little inputs, huge outputs.

Harsh and Brutal Corrections of Unwanted Behaviors

The flipside of giving players amazing juicy rewards is punishing them horrendously when they do something wrong. It is fine to punish players for things they have done incorrectly once they have learned to play, as I have said repeatedly. You might wonder, throughout this book, how games that are hard as nails and force you to die over and over again can be fun. Well, like *Contra* that I mentioned earlier, death doesn't have to be a negative experience so long as something is learned or gained from it. I would argue that a death that only brings you back a few minutes is worse in the learning design sense, as the designers aren't exactly sure when the player is going to die. In a good design, the only time players die is when they have made a mistake even though they had everything at their disposal not to. When this happens, go for it, open the floodgates, and let slip the most horrific punishments your sadistic mind can cook up. Murder their sidekick, delete their save file, burn their house down. You get the idea. So long as your punishments are backed up by learning support, and players feel like they deserved it, they will try again, littered though they may be with the ashes of their former home.

Rewards Must Scale in Their Splendor and Awesomeness

Games allow us to scale our rewards up, and up, and up. Everything we do can get more and more amazing the more times we do it. Unfortunately, this is not a representation of the real world, but it has a particular psychological benefit. The effect allows rewards not to get boring. In a standard behavioral stimulus-response chain, you would be giving someone a reward, but the reward would eventually become less and less enticing. In economics, this is called the effect of diminishing returns. Essentially, I can only bribe you with chocolates so many times until you want that chocolate less and less. Eventually, in fact, the chocolate will become a punishment as your stomach becomes full and you become progressively more nauseous. Games allow rich and varied rewards every single time a player does something, and this allows designers to make sure everything stays awesome all the time. Since this opportunity is available, there is no good reason not to do it. Make small actions have huge rewards all the time, and make them get bigger and bigger as players achieve more and more. *World of Warcraft* does this amazingly well. Another game we have mentioned that was great at it was *Mortal Kombat*. Tell me you didn't do uppercuts over and over again just to hear the guy yell *TOASTY!* Peppering amazing rewards throughout repeated tasks is one of the wonderful features of video games, and one of the things that makes them ideal for learning. Behaviorally, players can't get used to rewards the way they can in traditional learning, and you should use this to your advantage when designing the learning in your game.

Dynamic Difficulty Adjustment

This is something that teachers do instinctively or at least by training, after years and years of teaching hundreds of students. When it is apparent that a student is having trouble with a particular element of a problem, a teacher will use cognitive apprenticeship to scaffold his or her learning by offering advanced schemata to decode and chunk the problem down into bits that are more manageable. As the student develops his or her schema, the teacher will reduce the assistance until the student is capable on his or her own. How do we do this age-old teaching method in games? We detect player behaviors and respond accordingly. In the *Skull Island* example, enemy AI prioritized targeting friendly AI players until the player had successfully killed some of them. As the player became more and more proficient at slaughtering the enemies, the enemies stopped their prioritizing behavior. If the player suddenly and without warning starts doing horribly, the enemies will go back to deprioritizing the player. This effect fades after a certain number of enemies have been killed. I haven't conducted a study (yet) to figure out exactly what this number ought to be, but hopefully the point remains clear. We can scale our rewards through programming hooks when we know the player needs a hand. We can detect when players are dying in a certain area with something like a heat map, which is a map of where deaths or other important events occur, and then dynamically adjust the level design to reroute players to places where they will be met with more success. There are so many teaching tools at our disposal; it behooves us to learn to use them so that our players can enjoy our games to the greatest extent possible.

Test and Retest Player Skill Level

It takes a long time for things to move from short-term or working memory into long-term memory. We are not exactly sure how long this kind of thing can take to the second, but it is generally accepted that in good educational research, it is necessary to retest learners after they have been given some kind of learning treatment and then left alone for a while. In your game, it is important to keep up with learner play knowledge by making sure to constantly test the player. Teachers do this by re-applying numerous methods of validating learning, like tests, performances, speeches, and so on. In games, this means we need to continually increase difficulty, but occasionally present the player with older, easier tasks. This is done in an effort to check to see if the player's long-term memory has been altered by the teaching mechanics. If players are learning how to get farther in the game, but forgetting the fundamental mechanics, they are not far from becoming frustrated. For this reason, it is important to collect data on whether players retained information taught to them in the early tutorials, and respond accordingly with dynamic difficulty or rewards. In ensuring that players consistently have a high level of content knowledge, we will keep them in the flow channel and on task for the largest amount of time possible.

Use Just-in-Time Tactics to Reward Continued Play

As we have talked about, you can reinforce and remove behaviors with responses that are positive or negative. To this point, we've talked about these only in the context of culling or encouraging behaviors that correspond to game mechanics, but one further thing we can do with behavioral teaching methods is encourage people to keep playing. If we consider that playing itself is a behavior to be reinforced, we can use certain methods to make sure this happens. How might we do this? *World of Warcraft* does this with things like "rested experience." They reward the player for coming back to the game. This is exactly the kind of mechanic that keeps people playing, if *World of Warcraft*'s decade-long continuing success is any evidence of that fact. In our games, we want players to have rewards for signing back in. Give them items by surprise when they come back to the game just to thank them for doing it. This relates to our just-in-time conversation from previous chapters. We have no idea why the player turned the game off per se, so let's assume it is because the player got bored or frustrated. In this way, the reward for returning is a just-in-time treatment with the intention of keeping the player playing the game. You can wrap this in the game's mechanics. Make it so that the *Skull Island* explorers keep looking around the dungeon and give you amazing rewards every time you play. This system makes the players slowly associate starting the game with positive experiences. If we can work in mechanics like this, players are more likely to start our game just for the heck of it. I hope that this will get them involved in what they are doing, and keep them interested because our learning design is so amazing—right?

Procedural and Dynamic Rewards and Punishments

Just like our procedural and dynamic difficulty, we can also procedurally and dynamically generate rewards and punishments for players. This means using procedural algorithms to make new items, or procedural punishments to dynamically render you dying, kind of like seeing a flying foot in *Team Fortress 2*. You know you shouldn't have died, and the punishment is clear, but at the same time, you're having some fun. As I have discussed in other points, there is a diminishing returns effect that happens when you repeatedly do the same thing to players, good or bad. In *Skull Island*, the procedurally generated dungeon floors can be seen as a kind of procedural reward—getting to new floors gives you access to dungeons you have probably never seen before. To this end, you continue to be motivated to get deeper and deeper in the dungeon, and thus to keep playing. The more you get used to using behavioral incentives to keep players interested in your game's objectives, the more you'll get used to using these kinds of tactics to keep people playing at all.

You Cannot Have Too Many Data Collection Hooks

Many of the things we have discussed in this book rely on you having collected data to analyze. Much of the user research work done at numerous companies in the industry also relies on hooks like these. In fact, user research and usability departments are hard at work as we speak making a concerted effort to get more data collection methodologies in the game to make sure that they can perform amazing user research. In order to use methodologies like cognitive apprenticeship, you need to figure out where people's deficiencies lie. The only way to do this, of course, is to gather data. In the *Skull Island* example, the AI did not target players until they managed to kill an enemy. Furthermore, dungeons procedurally generated in ways that the players did not expect by examining their movement patterns. This kind of stuff makes games great. If you're not sure how these programming hooks might work, a good mantra is: there's no such thing as too much data. If you want to make every single player throw a huge chunk of data to a server every minute that contains health, level, gender, chosen character role, current money, quests completed, etc., that is amazing and useful. If it is a variable in your program, you should be recording it all the time.

Summary

I hope that this gives you some idea of how to collect data from your players and use them to make amazing learning experiences. It is so important in learning design to make sure that every learner is accommodated. If you take the time to rip out this chapter and staple it to the wall of your office, you'll have a better idea of how you're going to go about making people learn their way through your game.

I really hope you have enjoyed the book to this point and found it useful. If you have any questions about how you might do further research and learning, please don't hesitate to look me up, or check out the Further Reading section in the Appendix at the end of the book. Remember that human learning is happening every time someone picks up your game and starts playing it. What you want your players to learn and how you decide to make that happen is entirely up to you.

Appendix: Further Reading

In this appendix, I am going to outline all of the various stuff I have referenced throughout the book. My work is the result of the work of years of scholars before me, and I hope you will seek further knowledge in this area by looking up their work, buying their books, and reading, reading, reading.

Richard Mayer: Cognitive Theory of Multimedia Learning

Mayer's Cognitive Theory of Multimedia Learning forms the basis for a lot of the research I've done in my university and professional career. The theory contains well-wrought principles forged in years of research that support different methods of learning from multimedia. Many of these were illustrated throughout the book as game design principles. We only scratched the surface of the principles and the research supporting them, however. If you are interested in further reading on the topic, I would suggest picking up the following books:

Mayer, R. (2009). *Multimedia learning*. Boston, MA: Cambridge University Press.

Kalyuga, S. (2008). *Managing cognitive load in adaptive multimedia learning*. Hershey, PA: IGI Global.

Van Eck, R. (2010). *Gaming and cognition: Theories and practice from the learning sciences*. Hershey, PA: IGI Global.

Allan Paivio: Dual Coding Theory

Paivio's dual coding theory laid the groundwork for a huge number of later theories that would interrogate the difference between auditory and visual processing in human cognition. For this reason, it should be considered foundational reading for anybody interested in how humans learn from multimedia presentations like films, games, or animations. It can be very heavy at times, but if you are particularly interested in differences in audio and video processing, I'd check it out.

Paivio, A. & Sadoski, M. (2012). Imagery and text: A dual coding theory of reading and writing. New York: Routledge.

Bruce Mann: Attentional Control Theory

Attentional control theory is a less well-known but still influential theory on how the human mind acquires long-term information through gradual exposure to multimedia via the working memory. It prescribes particular uses for sound, which is its unique feature. Also rather psychologically heavy, this one can certainly be used to augment your understanding of the dual coding and cognitive theories of learning.

Mann, B. et al. (2012). Sustained learning in 4th and 5th graders but not 7th graders: Two experiments with a talking pedagogical agent. In Jiyou Jia (Ed.) *Educational stages and interactive learning: From kindergarten to workplace training*. Hershey, PA: IGI Global.

Classical Literature on Education

Much of what I have written in this book draws on classical educational literature, including the works of Vygotsky, Dewey, Skinner, and others. Included here are some of the classical references you might want to look up in order to get a better grasp on education as a whole.

Vygotsky, L. S. (1978). *Mind in society: The development of higher psychological processes*. Cambridge, MA: Harvard University Press.
Dewey, J. (1934). *Art as experience*. New York: Minton, Balch, & Company.
Skinner, B. F. (1957). *Verbal behavior*. Acton, MA: Copley Publishing Group.
Piaget, J. (1951). *The psychology of intelligence*. London: Routledge Publishers.

Of course, many of the classical works have been rewritten, summarized, and republished a million times over. Any of these books would be fine to get a good understanding of foundational educational theory, particularly considering how much I have crammed into this one book.

Allan Baddeley: Working Memory

Baddeley's working memory theory laid the framework for a lot of what we understand about how short-term memory is recoded into long-term memory over time. Many modern theories are based on Baddeley's original observations. If you desire a greater understanding of the learning taking place when a learner is seeing audiovisual presentations, and can't quite figure out how long-term memory works, this is a great place to start.

Baddeley, A. (1987). *Working memory*. Gloucestershire, UK: Clarendon Press.

Index